Together We Rise:

Voices from the Frontlines of Freedom

Anthology Rebelling against Injustice

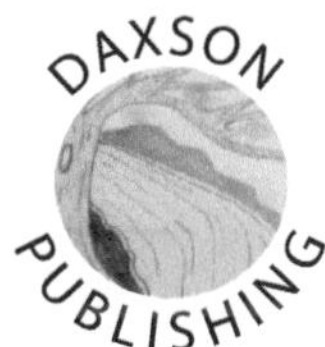

Together We Rise Voices from the Frontlines of Freedom

ISBN: 978-1-966337-33-1
Library of Congress Number: 2026902552

First Edition, © 2026

Printed in the United States of America

Edited by Cherice Cameron and Peter Lechuga
Cover Design by Erica Castro
Layout Design by Erica Castro

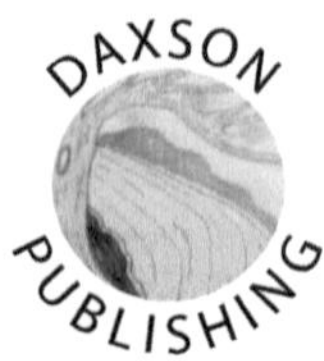

This books is dedicated to those who live with fear, hope, and love all in one moment. For those who have been separated from their loved ones, from their community, and from their safety. For those who never give up and stand in resistance through their art, photography, poetry, and manifestos you are giving voice to the voiceless..

We dedicate these pages to all of the people that have suffered and are still suffering due to these injustices. You are not alone. We see you and we stand with you.

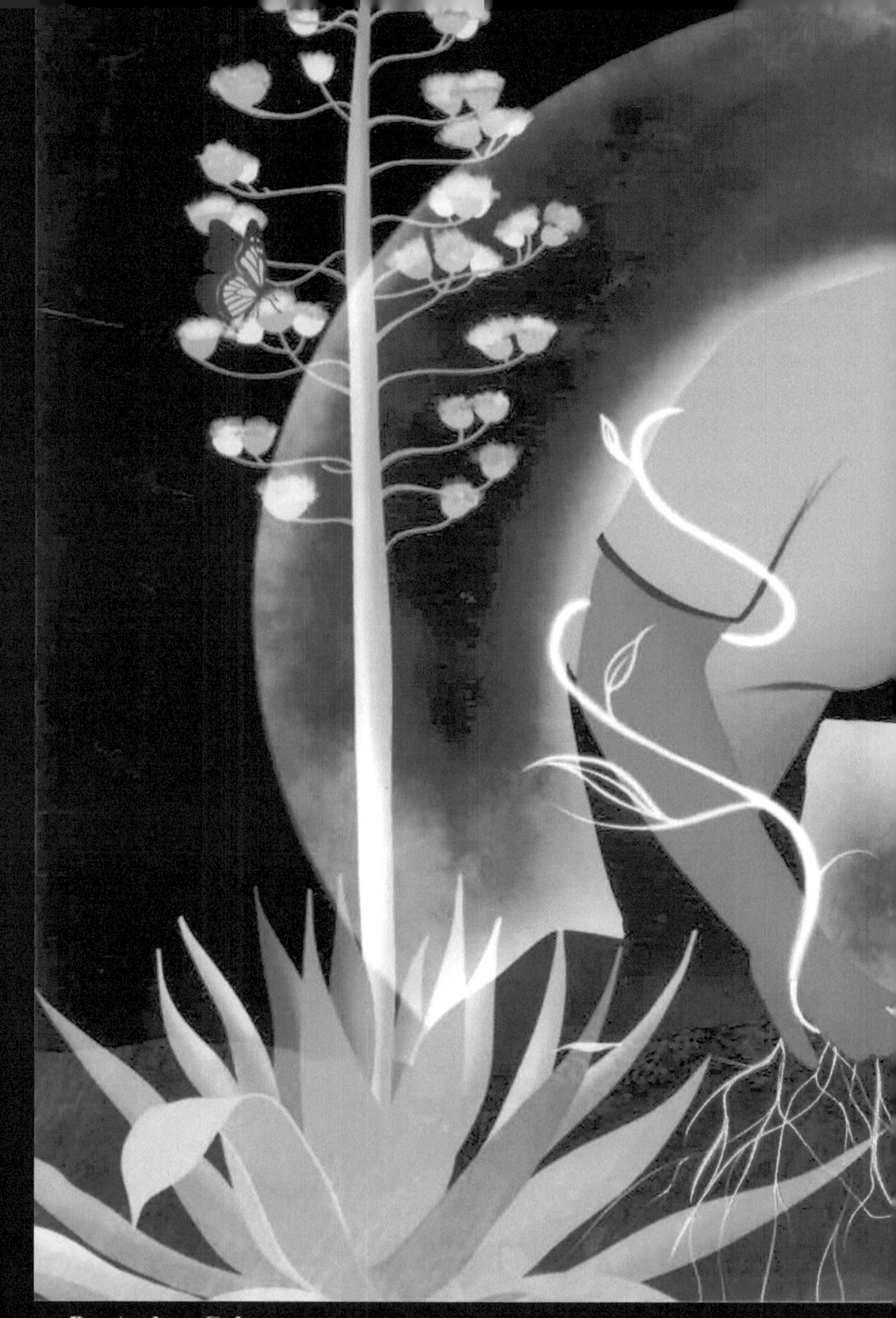

By: Andrea Galvez

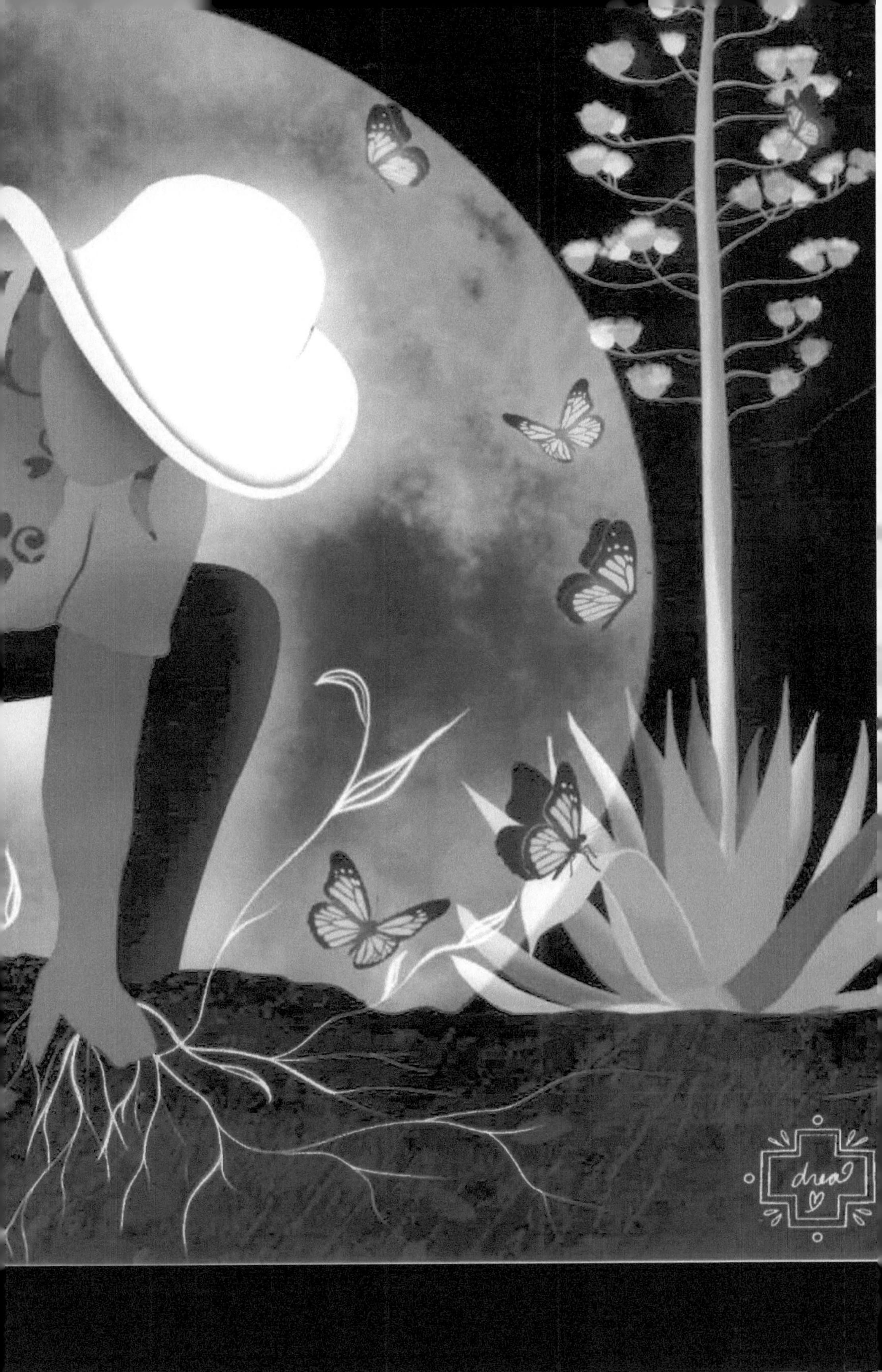

Editor's Note

When we came together as a team at Daxson Publishing to discuss the birth of *Together We Rise: Voices from the Frontlines of Freedom,* we decided that as artists it is time to stand united against the injustices wracking our country and our shared earth. As people of all ages are being ripped from homes, from streets that should be full of laughter, play, community, and care for humanity without bias. Without fear. Daxson Publishing put out the call to fellow artists and the response we received was unapologetic, alive in truth, humanity, and a desire to provide a historical account of the atrocities taking place at home and abroad.

Courage lives in this book. Nestled between pages of sorrow, disgust, terror, dismay, and unyielding bravery are moments of peace. Normalcy before, and after, the storm of human indignity. When ICE sweeps MacArthur Park and surrounding neighborhoods, **Carlos Ornelas** weeps along with the people of Olvera in his poem *ICE RAIDS* as "tears of black ink flood the streets of downtown." Where people shout "we will not go down without a fight," and artists take note and remember.

Look into the eyes of **Metzli Vik Villa's** photo of *resistance, revival*, as they stand with their sign that says *Chinga la Migra* protesting for peace. They are humanity standing at the gaping mouth of a monster in proclamation.

"If the Rarámuri can run 200 miles with bare feet

beyond that distance, can our resistance sing?

Yes! Our resistance sings! We will record and remember! Resist! Rebel! Write truth to battle lies!

In Peace We Stand,

Cherice Cameron

Poet – Artist – Musician – Activist

Editor's Note

Together We Rise: Voices from the Frontlines of Freedom was born in a summer of sirens, a season of separating families, an age of aggression and absence, and a period of people coming together, building community, and resisting.

This anthology is an act of resistance. It is a fist in the air blooming a middle finger to this administration. It is stories of families merely trying to exist in a time when a portion of this country hates us simply for existing.

As you look through the writings and art in this collection you will find reflections echoing the symphony of neighborhoods, children playing on the street, the gleeful honk of the paletero, the songs that our parents used to sing to us, and the chants of a united front defying fascism.

In Solidarity,

Peter Lechuga

Poet – Editor – Activist

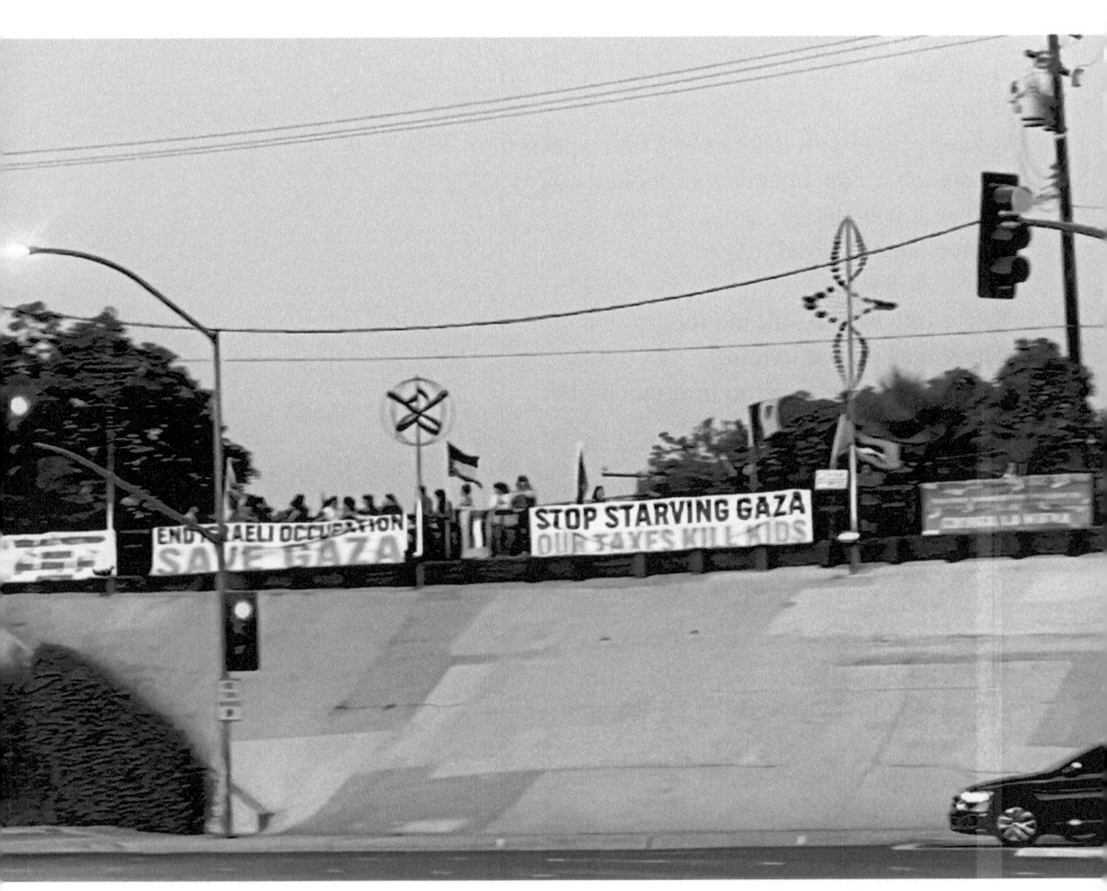

By: Dante Castro Lopez

For Renee Nicole Good

My heartbeat is not a war drum.
It is a witness.
It stutters.
It breaks.
It keeps time with a street in Minneapolis
where a woman's name was spoken once
before it was taken.
Renee Nicole Good.
Say it slowly.
Say it like breath still matters.
There was no battlefield.
No smoke, no sirens, no mutual combat.
Only a street,
a car,
a body startled by men who arrived
already rehearsing violence.
They called it enforcement.
They called it protocol.
They called it fear turned righteous.
But fear fired first.
Renee Nicole Good was not a weapon.
She was not an operation.
She was not a threat.
She was a mother.
A poet.
A citizen of breath and language.
A woman who did not lower her eyes
when power demanded obedience.
That was her crime.
My heart cannot hold this.
There is no language thick enough
to carry a bullet and call it law.
No prayer clean enough
to rinse blood from a badge.
This grief has weight.
It leans into the body.
It bends the knees of everyone
who knows the difference
between safety and domination.
They want us to argue policy.
They want us to debate borders.

They want the conversation to stay abstract
so the dead stay quiet.
But this is not theory.
This is a woman shot in the street
by agents trained to see enemies
where neighbors live.
This is what happens
when empire forgets how to recognize humanity.
Renee Nicole Good had a child
who will learn her name
through absence.
A family who will set an extra place
and never stop setting it.
The earth remembers this.
The pavement remembers.
The air that left her lungs
has not forgiven.
ICE is not just an acronym.
It is a method.
It is cold made official.
It is the logic that says some lives
can be ended for efficiency.
Minneapolis knows it now.
So does Albuquerque.
Standing Rock knew it.
Pine Ridge.
Chiapas.
Everywhere power wears a uniform
and calls itself inevitable.
They kill with bullets.
We answer with memory. With heart.
We answer by refusing to forget
the sound of her name.
Renee Nicole Good.
We answer by grieving out loud.
By standing in streets that were never meant
to be execution grounds.
By holding our rage carefully,
like fire meant to warm, not erase.
There is no neutrality here.
There is no safe distance
from a burning house.
Silence sides with the gun.
We are not afraid of your weapons.

We are afraid of numbness.
We are afraid of becoming fluent
in looking away.
So we plant marigolds.
We say her name.
We tell our children
this should never have happened
and we mean it.
And someday,
the land will soften.
The blood will dry.
The lies will crack.
And the dead will be remembered
not as casualties
Not as victims
but as teachers
As mothers
As poets.
Until then,
we keep saying her name.
Renee Nicole Good.
As a vow.
We will breathe together.
We will mourn together.
And we will not let her disappear.
Not now.
Not ever.

By: Manuel Gonzalez
New Mexico's Poet Laureate

ICE RAIDS

Today ice rode through McArthur park
during rush hour.
They came with Humvees and trucks and Humvees and trucks
and horses.
Helicopters Cameramen.
On a huge convoy of wasted tax dollars.
It was all some kind of show
the mayor Karen Bass showed up
and was conveniently on the phone on live stream
talking to someone and called off ICE.
This was all a show.
This was a symbol of power.
White power.

This was a show of power by a white supremacist America.
A corrupt trump regime drunk off the grapes of wrath in the euphoria of power.
A business scoundrel arrogant bigot scourge of the political scene and the mad evil scientist inventor billionaire, a white African fiend.

It is day 32 or 33 of the ice raids, I lost count.
Peter handed me a stick
and I busted the head off an ICE pinata,
candy spills all over San Bernardino.
Ice is taking my people . . .
And I can't cry . . .
My pen cries for me.
Tears of ice.
Tears of black ink
flood the streets of downtown,
placita Olvera,
to let the world know
that we were here,
we resisted,
we protested,
we wrote.
And this is not over,
we will not go down
without a fight.

By: Carlos Ornelas

Sabrina's on the Radio Again

God is on the radio
and he's reading our prayers out loud
but no one listens to the radio anymore

if someone does its just fat greasy fingers
turning the knob until it changes to the
same endless Sabrina Carpenter song.

as long as there's a pretty blonde girl under the spotlight
they can ignore the not so pretty brown
girls being taken off the street.

girls that still carry an accent
girls who have only ever known the streets of Los Angeles
girls running errands for their mothers

As LA set downs it cinematic sunset on its star-studded streets
Are the mothers standing at their porches?
clutching a rosary, a bible, a phone with 20 missed calls

do they regret all their prayers for a healthy pretty baby
and wish they prayed for an unassuming ugly child?

Is ugliness enough protection from dirty hands?

if it is,
then where are our girls?
not found in Southgate, or Lincoln Heights, or Van Nuys, or Pacoima
they are not in school or in clinics getting vaccines
not getting raspados under crystal sunlight.

our girls are not as blonde and red-lipped
as sweet little Sabrina Carpenter.
no names on shiny billboard lights.
just a single name filling someone's quota.
a quota fulfilling a darker kind of prayer
uttered by stone lips
a prayer that what must be dark must be kept away.
swept and hidden under radio music
no one really listens to anymore.

it always plays the same song afterall.

By: Hope Cerna

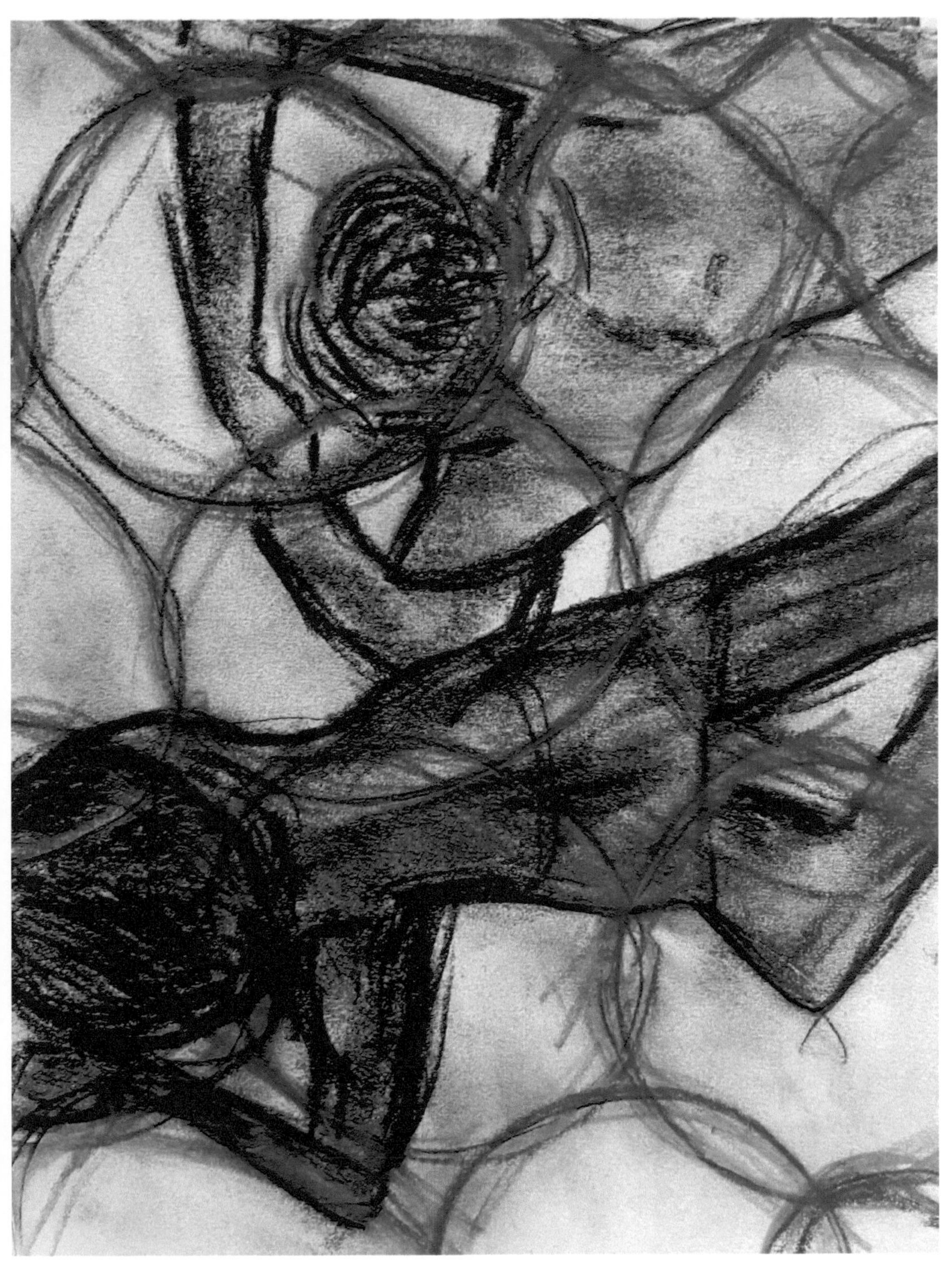

By: Gina Rae Duran

DISAPPEARED

if I share my location
on my way to work
because of that post
because I called it what it is
madness, murder, hate
demanding a warrant
an article I co-authored
for our student paper
saying words like
genocide, Gaza, manslaughter
civilians, West Bank
on my college campus
disappeared
on a crowded street corner
after a judge approved my stay
my way to break bread
after fasting for worship
on my way to service
at a construction site
know your rights card ready
unmarked prejudice
car windows rolled up
if I am from this land

waiting on my lawyer
shattered car window
broken glass in my baby's car seat
son left standing on the curb
pregnant wife by my side
where I study nuclear physics
PHD bound this summer
on a plane to El Salvador
on a train to Texas
called a terrorist
coming back from vacation
if my partner took me to see the ocean
whereabouts unknown
five men to one
while my children at school
onlookers filming
my mother wailing
zip tie my wrists
birth certificate in hand
plain clothes kidnapping
on a Saturday afternoon
when will I know
the safety of home

By: Azalea Aguilar

THERE ARE NO WRONG DECADES
ONLY THOSE DOING THE WRONGING

Land of opportunity
is actually
land of chance
to be born
in the wrong decade
one where you're
gassed up in gasoline baths
or
encaged by Juan Crow
or
operated by Operation Wetback
or
stripped of your Zoot Suits
or
one

where you are detained
when you should feel enraged
you are free to speak
just not ill against their president
their idol
their dictator

Dear leader,
I fear
no king
no God

especially if you is all you got

Send your army wielding untouchable and invincible

it's happening again

just the armor is a little bit different

the name isn't Cortez

but the blood runs imperialism

Conquest means kidnapping

ICE means melt

Resist means rise

Protest means people

I mean us

I mean we

I mean we deserve

respect

so do

the Papi's in neon long sleeves enduring sunshine every day

to sow beautiful pastures that once yielded fields of fruit

so do

the Mami's bussing it in pristine uniforms to El Toro,

Northgate, El Super, but she is the real Superior one

so do

Las señoras—hood abuelitas—limping with reusable bags not meant to be reused, carrying plastic bottles to be recycled

for income condensed into cubes fit into pockets

pinched for misa, for masa, por más

un poco más

so do

Los señores—hood abuelitos—pushing raspados o mangos o nieve or ringing sweet sounds of summer echoing, beckoning, inviting all to gather over glistening joy to marvel how we made it this far

so do

Los niños,

nuestros niños,

robbing their tongue, now their loved ones.

When will it ever be enough?

When their use is gone, they are called anchors

doomed to drown after being thrown overboard

so do

Our hermanos y hermanas trans

our siblings who have suffered outside of the family

let us make sure home is where they are welcome

to take up space

to be safe

to be loved

I digress

this isn't progress

this is regress

this isn't a mistake

this is their play

remember the U.S. modeled what Nazis would do

it's only returning the favor

Por favor

No more

Let this night lower its knives

Let this match light the new day

Let this brick guide my throw

Let us

keep us safe

By: Alexis Jaimes

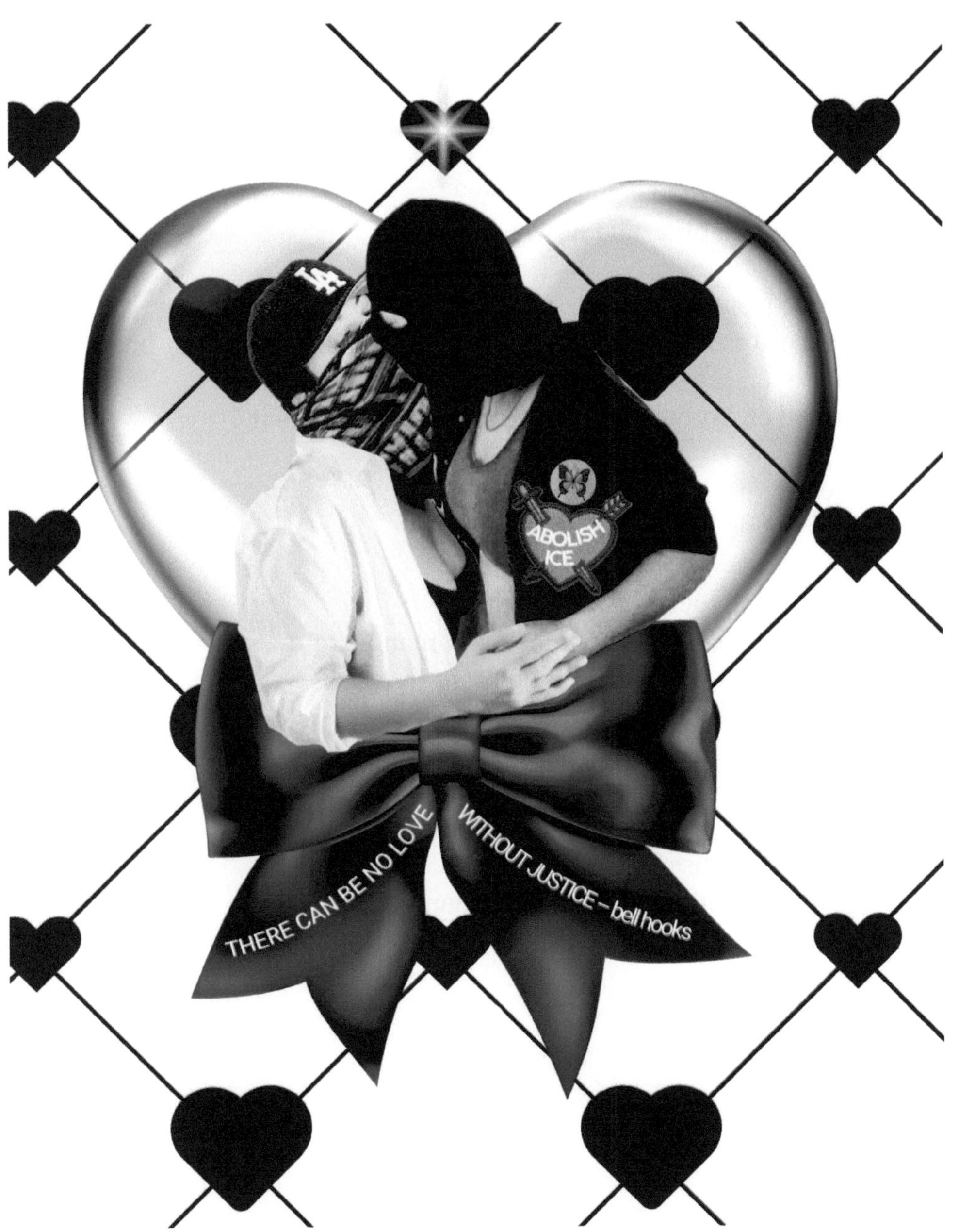

By: Anna Goodman Herrick

Love Poem #2

Earrings sheath in palms like swords
Ancient rituals in preparation for war
She asks, “Do I have to get crazy now?”
Skies erupt in red, blue, and howls

“Did that pig just racial profile you?
Saw the ancestors haunt your skin, the mountains peak in your hue?
Pulled you over, praying you sang in an accent
Pulled you over, knowing the government commands it.”

Our bodies are not quotas
Our bodies are devoted

Exposed tradition locked in a glove box
Hoops ceased to dangle, hands meant to mangle, gloves off
A woman with her hair up, nothing more righteous
Her tongue more blunt than all of their nightsticks

And I fell in her words and truly desired
All squad cars cleansed in holy bonfires
Stars gaze back, count the twinkling phantoms
Become sunrise in glass, Immolate in passion

Because
Our bodies are not quotas
Because
Our bodies are devoted

By: Peter Lechuga

From a Window

Lights are falling from the sky
and all I can think about
is how pretty they are

Maybe they are falling stars.
maybe it's God's tears
reminding us he's there.
maybe it's all a dream.

I wish it was a dream
when those falling stars
reveal themselves to be missiles.

War tastes different
when its no longer framed
in a political cartoon
an old textbook
or a scrolling headline

I watch as humans
destroy other humans
from someone else's iphone footage.

In this footage
people with hair as dark as mine
watch with eyes as brown as mine
stand at their balcony window
as missiles trail though the
night sky like little white shooting stars

Was it dinner time? A birthday celebration with
the windows opened wide to let the night breeze in?
does the night air smell of smog like in LA?

I feel the impact of these shooting stars
at the same time they do.

I always thought myself an honest person
but god did the lies
bubble up on my tongue so quickly.
so fast. all to choke me away from this footage
that somehow popped up on my For You Page.

the sweet lie…
that this isn't real
this can't be real

not because it's so easy
to fake video nowadays,
that A.I tricks us better each day
and I've never seen a missile
beyond a hollywood frame so how can I
know a real missile from a scripted one?

No, I tell myself the most naive lie of all
this can't be real
because what living man could
decide to hit the button on those missiles?
what living creature could be borne by a woman
skin childish knees, eat summer fruit
and still decide–
to do that?

On the other side of the world
I keep scrolling my phone
make a vet appointment for my cat,
eat apples,
watch my brother leave for a friday night out
and get ready for bed early
I lie
I sleep
I write
and I think of those shooting stars

Did the children think they were shooting stars?
watching from their window at night
Did they make a wish on those stars?

By: Hope Cerna

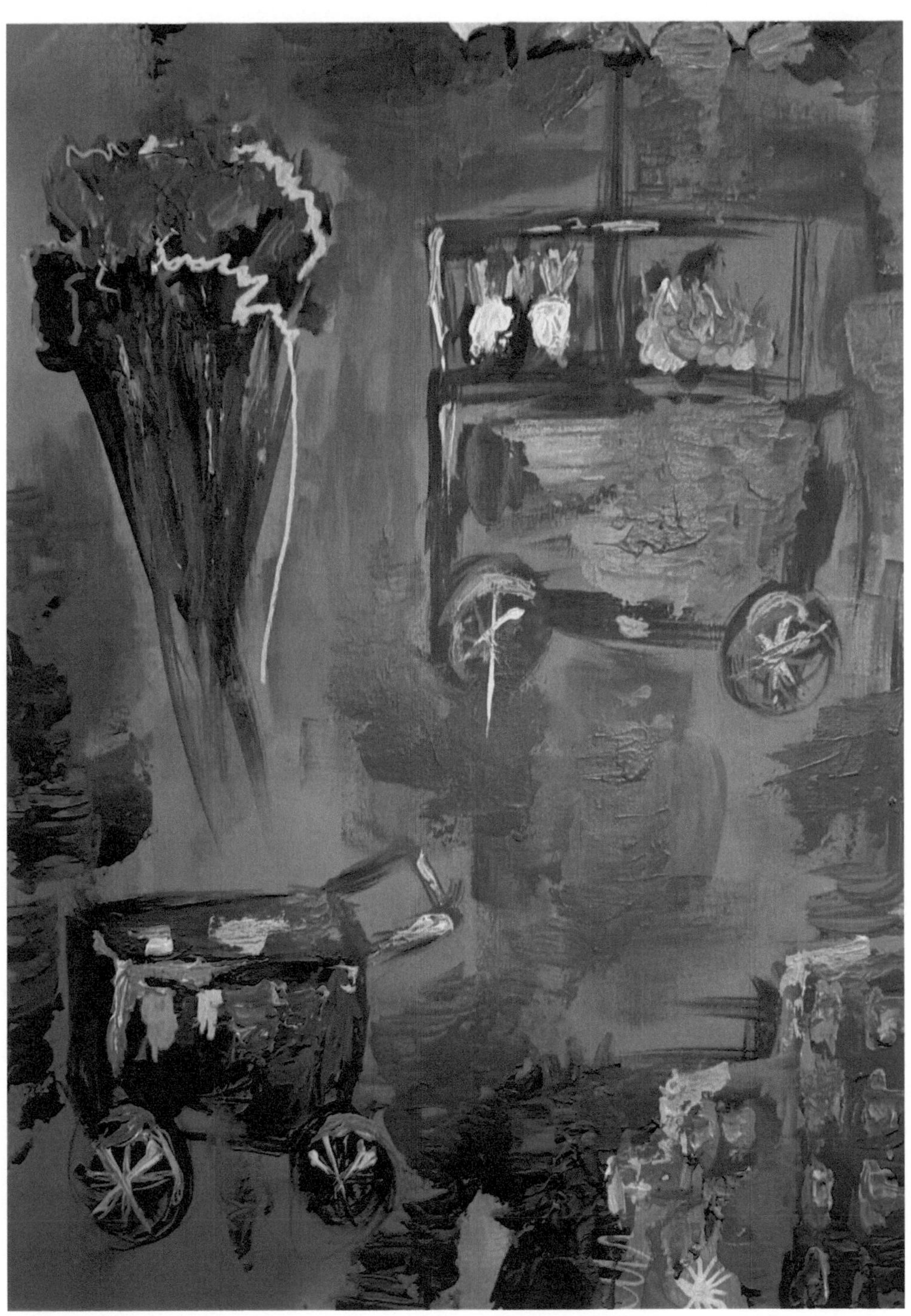

By: Alejandra J. Lopez

A Borderless Imagination

It's time to imagine a world without borders.
In the U.S. today, legal immigration is in shambles. Visas are all over the place and confusing (different visas for different countries, circumstances, where even big money can buy you a visa). Asylum seekers, a legitimate way to be allowed into the country, are being pulled from federal buildings and deported. People who have for years lawfully reported to immigration authorities are now in detention. Those who have worked in the country for decades, raised children, bought houses, paid taxes, and helped the economy with their labor or businesses, have been snatched away by masked ICE agents or bounty hunters. Even citizens have been detained and/or deported.

Whatever due process existed (it's always been bad) is gone now.
Getting legal status? There was never a "line" to begin with. Prior to Trump, Mexicans averaged around twenty years to obtain legal status (and this with a relative in the U.S. helping their application). For those from the Philippines it's around twenty-five years.
That's all out the window.

I know about this. For several years in the 2000s and 2010s, I helped immigration law firms on over one hundred asylum cases for people facing gang or cartel violence in Mexico and Central America. We lost many cases, but the ones we won saved lives. Believe me, it was a maze even then.
Around the world, for most of this century and the last, if you sought a better life in another country, whether because of war, poverty, discrimination, famine, or eco-disasters, you had to become a refugee, undocumented, or die.
We've been imprisoned by the nation state.

Nation-states are a relatively new historical concept. Before "nations" were established in Europe and other parts of the world there were kingdoms, fiefdoms, dynasties, empires, caliphates, communities, peoples, or tribes. Following the Thirty-years' War, a largely Catholic versus Protestant calamity, in which some eight million people were killed, the Holy Roman Empire with the kingdoms of France and Sweden, and their respective allies, signed the 1648 Peace of Westphalia, a complicated drawn-out process that introduced the idea of state sovereignty, whereby each state could govern its own people and territory without external interference.

In the late 1700s to early 1800s, the United States and other western hemispheric countries that emerged from Spanish, English, and French colonial rule provided models for global nation building.Nationalism arose during the French Revolution emphasizing a people with shared identity and allegiance. Later Napoleon

utilized this nationalism to conquer and reorganize much of Europe. This in turn sparked nationalist sentiments in places he subdued. Within a decade or more after Napoleon's defeat, new nations born in Europe included Italy, Belgium, Greece, and Germany. The concept of "nation" expanded to include shared culture, language, and history, all of which turned around the development of home markets. With the collapse of the Ottoman Empire after World War I, and later the British empire among others, new nations emerged in Europe as well as the Mid-East, Africa, Asia, and parts of Latin America. Today the globe has been divided into some 195 sovereign states.
Because of this mostly random creation of "nations," borders and peoples didn't fall neatly into a "common" category. Wars, annexations, land-buys, and empire dissolution created weird boundaries and unconnected communities into one so-called nation.

The United States is no exception.
Take my family. I was born in 1954 in El Paso, Texas when we lived in Ciudad Juarez, Mexico. This area along with parts of New Mexico and Arizona, as well as Chihuahua and other Mexican states, are in the Chihuahuan Desert. My mother had roots with the Rarámuri people (also known as the Tarahumara) who have been on this desert, along with other original peoples, for tens of thousands of years. To have me, my mother crossed the International Bridge between the two cities. At the time, the U.S/Mexico border had only been there 106 years. She went from "our land to our land."

There are U.S. tribes like the Tohono O'odham and Kumeyaay who have lands and people in both Mexico and the United States. Because of our Indigenous ties to Nahuas, Mayans, Zapotecos, Mixtecos, Purépecha, Pipil, and others, most Mexicans and Central Americans aren't foreigners or strangers—even if we're treated as such.

The Trump Administration's recent deportation raids have targeted people from all over, but the vast majority are brown-skinned, indicative of their Indigenous ancestry. From June 1 of this year in the Los Angeles area alone, ICE detained over 1,600 people. From previous reports, 70 percent had no criminal convictions. Around 75 percent were from Mexico, Guatemala, Honduras, and El Salvador.

The United States, a relatively new country, became an industrial and financial powerhouse without the hindrance of a feudal system. Yet, two things helped make this country "great': First, *free land* stolen in all manner of ways from Indigenous peoples but also relatively cheap land purchases and outright invasions (under the color of "manifest destiny") including half of Mexico and all of Puerto Rico. Secondly, *free labor*—a system of Black chattel slavery that existed since before its beginning and culminated in major enterprises such as cotton, tobacco, shipping, textiles, banking, and more.

The foundation of who we are as a country was built on these two "freedoms." Today the United States is a prison house of nations with 574 federally recognized tribal nations (and many non-federally recognized peoples). Also, cultural, social, and political differences in various parts of the country such as the South, Northeast, Midwest, Pacific Northwest, and Southwest (mostly the old Mexico section). I've been around the whole country and these differences are palpable. You can also add the specific histories and cultural roots of states like Hawai'i and Alaska or territories like Guam, American Samoa, or the Virgin Islands.

All this makes for a rich land, a diverse and wondrous garden of peoples, histories, and tongues. To pretend we are one nation with one history, one culture, or one set of principles, is social erasure and a denial of our multiple entanglements.

The right-wing, especially the White Christian Nationalists, want us to believe we are a "white" nation, founded on Christianity, and will do anything they can, legal or otherwise, to impede Black, Indigenous, and other communities of color from advancing. They also don't care about whites who are poor and working class, often women, or Queer and Trans. They've lied about everything, including history and cultural contribution.
Who needs any of this?

To live without these fabricated nations and borders, we can follow the natural order of the planet and human migration. For Mother Earth there are no borders. She welcomes anyone who walks her soils, lays down, swims, or dances. She doesn't care about skin color, whether one is straight, Queer, or trans, or what our belief system may be. We all matter in our distinctiveness, our unique qualities, our independent identities, but still with a common thread of love and liberation for all. Mother Earth does not care about states, armies, and geo-political interests. We are all inhabitants of a blue/green/cloudy world, not like the school maps with made-up colors and lines for nations, states, and provinces.

To Mother Earth, we all belong.

Also, migration is the human condition. For millions of years, our species has traveled from its birthplace in Africa to most corners of the world. Today, however, the natural state of migration has been criminalized.
Let's start with the rooted reality we all have in common, then go from there.
I'll explore this further in other blogposts, including specific details of how this borderless vision may be realized.

By: Luis J. Rodriguez

My Chicano Guardian Angel

My Chicano guardian angel lives through me
He's Generations deep guiding me through the streets
He reaffirms I may not be brown but this lighter shade is graced around town

Our jam WARS, "Don't let nobody get you down"
My Chicano guardian Angel protects me
He puts me in the right aisle to find the corduroy Dickies
He suggests I top it off with a black & white T.
He watches over me even when I was in County.
I go through the terrain for his side quests
To mirror justice, to collect debts,
Pay my respects in order to let the O.G. rest.
My Chicano Guardian Angel discerns the alley cats,
The fiends and the ones who pledge allegiance to
The Jezebel Queen.
My Chicano Guardian angel has lived through the drama & the trauma
To set me apart for one reason
My heart.

By: Aruj Khan

“Jaguar/Eagles”

The Brown Berets
the jaguars of today
a shot in the dark,
Laguna Park 1970
a shark sent in the LAPD with billy clubs
a monster with sub-human like syndromes
but we stood strong in *Califaztlan*
heart for our gente,
love for Vietnam,
Kiiz *Tamoanchan*
Tonantzin's song and serpent skirt,
defiant Brown shirts,
calling them locas,
because you can’t spell scholar without “chola”
vatos locos
to fierce *ocelotls*
the eagle warriors developed
in the chambers of *Tenochtitlan*
in order to melt that hielo
Atlachinolli, Huehueteotl
The Brown Berets
the honored eagles of today, the *Cuauhtzintli,*
training in the *telpochcalli.*
ce, ome, yei, nahui.
self defense by any means
necessary submissions of the body
and mind
legs and arms locked on time
Muay Thai striking sharp in the dark
and trenches,
playing the harp of *Xicana*
resistance critical *Panche be*
insistence
each one teach one
the people the Sun
the daughters of the earth
the militant tios for the little ones
and all they’re worth
Teoxihuitl, Chalchihuitl,
turquoise and jade
the rays of the son say

By: Tezozomoc

LA LLAMAN KINGSLAYER

As if it were a bad thing
As if respect means bowing down

When the crown calls their pawns
She says,
I'll show you mine if you show yours first–
Talkin' taxes
Because Dear Leader does not pay his

but
la señora selling elotes sin papeles does
the one who works
every day
every hour
without PTO
or 401K
or OSHA
or paid breaks
or dull, water cooler conversations on Tuesday afternoons shivering frostbite in first world AC

she pleads not for a tower with her name
but clean and warm water for her children
and toasty tortillas every morning
with time to make them
hecho de manos limpias
on the garden of her mandil
wiped clean
of laws
of bigots
of Nazis

she tells them
que se vayan a la chingada

then brags to the padre in the confession booth what she told them racist bastards
it's worth the 10 Ave Marias and 25 Padre Nuestros
just so her knuckles can savor the splintered teeth
she tore off the mad king
like he tore up the constitution of el barrio
the unwritten law that reads
you don't target the most vulnerable
because
when you do,
you pull apart the earth and
when you do,
you grant permission to be swallowed whole

By: Alexis Jaimes

Tired

I'm tired of sending letters,
Of signing petitions.

I'm tired of
Of asking my government
To save my life,
To save my friends lives,

Save the lives
Of people I don't know
People I've never met,
I'm tired of screaming
On the internet.

I'm tired of
Posting go-fund me
links online
Like it'll save the world.

I'm tired of
Calling governors
Who couldn't care less.
Congressmen who leave us on read.

I'm tired of inboxes full
Of tired people begging for help.

I'm tired of watching
Preventable crisis
After preventable crisis,
Mishandled,
Misconstrued,
By powerful people
Who just weren't in the mood,
To do more, to say more,
To stop more.

I'm tired of writing grant applications,

Of competing for help,
Of proving that I'm deserving of care.

I'm tired of donating to nonprofits,
That embezzle funds
But won't pay their workers
A livable wage.

Liberation may not happen
In my lifetime,
But could it speed up a little?

My friends are dying,
The planet's dying,

Sent, and delivered.

By: Milo Santamaria

resistance, revival

David Huerta was pushed, struck on the head to the ground,
tased, & arrested in front of the Edward Roybal building.
Huerta, a Latino labor leader,
the President of the Service Employees International Union,
leading 750,000 union members to support workers across California
in education, nursing, the social sector, the state government –
& to become US citizens

Roybal, the first Latino in the 20th century to be elected
onto LA City Council & the US House of Representatives,
a tenacious voice for health & advancement in our communities
for over four decades, from 1949 to 1993.

1993, the year i was born into 5 generations of Los Angeles Mexican-Americans,
from Kohler street in Downtown,
to Calzona in Boyle Heights,
to 3rd/Rowan in East Los,
to the Borderlands of Monterey Park.
my feet walk sensing our roots,
recognizing the escalated obstacles today's immigrants face
that undeniably break them down & reduce opportunities.

around us now are not deportations, but: **disappearances**.
taken are not invaders, but: **refugees, families** denied due process & **citizens.**

BEING UNDOCUMENTED IS NOT A CRIME
…especially as the government ends TPS, revokes student visas exercising freedom of speech to Free Palestine, threatens birthright citizenship, & removes legal status from people who "did it the right way" – y sabes que?!

¡CHINGA LA MIGRA!
¡FREE FAMILIES!
BEING BROWN OR BLACK IS NOT A CRIME.
ARMED KIDNAPPING IS A FELONY.

VIOLATING THE CONSTITUTION SHOULD
IMPRISON THE FELON PRESIDENT.
– yet 25+ states stand with 47 calling on the National Guard & the marines,
& mouths under red hats shout for martial law & wave confederate flags
while demonizing *us* as violent.

David Huerta was pushed, struck on the head to the ground,
tased, & arrested in front of the Edward Roybal building.

historic leaders of our comunidad
eclipsed together in a burst of true violence.

our leaders are waterfalls,
channeling all the sorrow & strife of our rivers
purifying our present, forming our future,
generating ripple effects – pebble by pebble – of many more like us:
to cure our societies of deep self-hatred,
to become advocates for change
& no, not to be victims –
or "sensitive snowflakes" or "libtards" —
to be survivors, believers, paradigm shifters.

¡venga! strike our head.
take down US Senator Alex Padilla to the ground
during his right to pose questions at a press conference,
& handcuff him? we'll curse you back off-the-cuff,

you are unprepared for our rough, ancient fortitude.

¡orale! call us rude? nah, we always renew.

no longer survival, we thrive in our revival.
our waterfalls cleanse & crash with our permanence.

my own resistance song unearths historia from my Grandma Juana,
a pillar in my family who held tenderly our heritage.

my percussion follows the wheels of the Model T. Ford
that drove my Grandma Juana's familia Silva
to Los Angeles from La Isla,
a small hill, within a valley of dry land,
with only one square of sidewalk.

my melodies beg for the abandoned piano
left in my grandma's grandma's
adobe house, la Casa de Sara Moraga,
remembered by Grandma Juana
as being dark & beautiful,
dressed in a skirt always long
& her hair always in long braids.

my heels *juana* beat against the mud,
as my short brown fingers dabble against the piano keys
striving for the harmonies
of my spirit, my heart, my fury

– yearning to release burned languages from buried ancestries:
Nahua, Comanche, Rarámuri…

if the Rarámuri can run 200 miles with bare feet,
beyond that distance, can our resistance sing?

By: Metzli Vik Villa

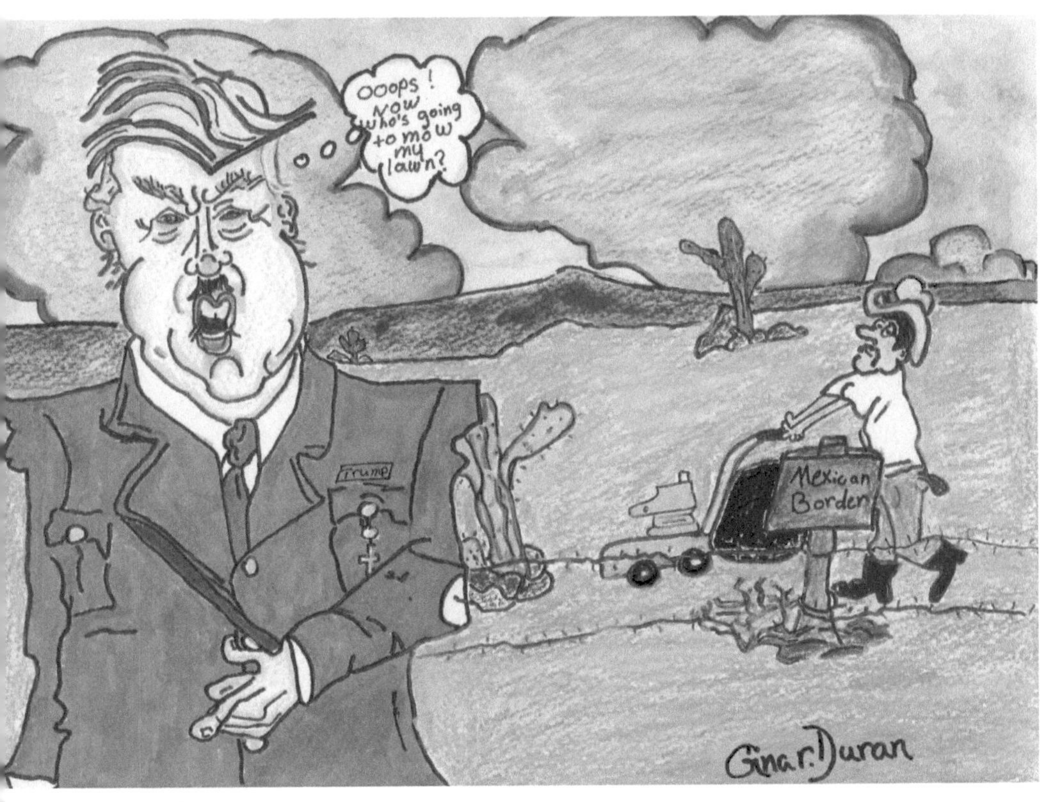

By: Gina Rae Duran

When ICE Sits Down for dinner
Previously published in the ILL Anthology Vol. III

When ICE sits down for dinner
Do they gather round the table
Are the children called in from playing
Fold hands for praying
Give thanks for food
Do they talk about their day
How it went, what lessons learned
No talk of those they preyed on
Then feast on boiled potatoes
Braised carrots
Sautéed green beans
Garden salad

When ICE sits down for dinner
After a long day of kidnapping children
Disappearing fathers trying to make a living
Stealing mother's planting flowers
Shoved into dark unmarked cars
Their bidding in black masks
What does mother serve them
That hasn't been picked by brown hands
Extracting these hands needed
Kneading dough for tortillas
Bite the hand that feeds them Birria
Immigrant hands sown seeds in
Fertile soil
Broken skin that bleeds from toil
Can they taste their sweat mixed in
The after taste of Mexican Braceros brought here to help when needing them
Every dry good that lines the shelf
Carries the labor of a close neighbor
Every bite at dinner savored
Every plate from kitchen to table
Its flavor
Criticizes ICE behavior for just doing a job
ICE can't have their cake and eat it too
Either immigrants are wanted or they're not
Treated like burros in the field
Measured only by proximity to the work they fill
We'll take their Churros, their Alote, their bacon wrapped dogs
Then send em back like perros
Blue colar heros
Less than human

Machinery
Mechanic
Line cook
Factory worker
Day laborer
The invisible made visible by orange reflective vests
Say they're physiologically designed for this
Clay figures of a Mexican at siesta
Redlined into Barrios
Con fuerza
Pushed face down into jobs a cracker don't fuck with
Cuz white skin burns easily
Turnt up white colars work easier

When ICE sits down for dinner
Every bite is a contradiction
Fork and knife dont go together
Their family's never had it better
On a tax payers salary immigrants have paid into

By day, they rob themselves of those they depend on
By night, they forget what they heard on Sunday
Love thy neighbor as thy self
Bless the hands that grew your food
Washed your car on Monday
Turned back your bed on vacation
Pumped your gas in stations
Brewed your coffee at 7/11
Raspberry Slurpees for your children
Every stud in the house you live in
Erected by those you round up on weekends
Each nail you depend on
Hang your tactical belt on
Established a home on
The table you eat on
Now want them all gone
Never realize
Zip ties made by the hands you brutalize
You crossed a border to get here

When ICE sits down for dinner
To wind down, the end of their day
Kids in from play
Does the family pray to a savior
Once a regal alien child in Eygpt
Or have they conveniently forgotten that narrative

Their lives are ill gotten
Dinning on the rotten assumptions
That folks can be illegal
That they are merely needed
Essential brown jobs
Always stealing white jobs
Valued for their employment
Cheap labor is their enslavement
Send em back to where they came from
The Domino effect of who's next
Show me your papers
A Real ID Card database
What'd you expect
When the lines so long
Your number never comes up
Doors always shut
Its easier to swim and turn dollars to pesos
ICE never had it so hard tho
Never forced to climb fences
Never stood by the river watching lights from El Paso
When deciding to cross is the best of two choices
Whispering voices calling for coyotes

When ICE sits down for dinner
They enjoy the freedom others have paid for
Fat salary bonus buys more
Filet Minon from the butcher, the real chingon
Jesus pushes a mower cross your OC front yard
In church on Sunday, rosary fumbled through mama's fingers
Kids down the block throwing rocks through ICE cruisers
Waiving the Mexican flag, chanting Chinga la Migra
Some will never make it home for dinner

By: Anonymous1

2025

The wood is on fire,
As I look deep into your eyes of blue and recall
“Our Better Angels” and wonder where she is,
As I remember to be human
To be kind and to be a creature of love.
To be a man holding on to love,
And loving so deeply that there is a place where the hate cannot go
As the Nazi paint infects the skin.
The skin of those who fear the others
Who fear me because I will not be silent
To the way they treat her.
It hurts inside to think she who is my wood and my world
Is left broken and torn sitting in the field struggling to find a voice
That will bring hope to the hopeless divide

And the wood is on fire,
But her people are not dead
Even if she’s changing in the dark,
As her moon is eclipsed by the voices of the hunters.
Yet, if I wait for just a moment in this moment
I can still see in her the good that cannot be taken
As the darkness also must pass

By: Conor Keating

Just Down My Street

There I lay, convalescent in my bed
while I heard a million helicopters overhead.

Sirens pierced through ear and heart
while ICE turned Home Depot into its mark.

The raids were down the street, so near.
as friends and family lived in fear.

I was stuck at home, confined to my bed
while those being kidnapped were left for dead.

Bounty hunters were taking people away
while all I could do was cry and pray.

Alone and distraught, trying to heal
as my neighbors worried about their next meal.

My friend and his family decided to leave
while I sat in horror, unable to conceive.

My heart was so broken with so much despair
while I implored the gods to end this nightmare.

I look back at this moment in utter disbelief
as I write about the ICE raids just down my street.

By: Diosa Xochiquetzalcóatl

Autopsy Report

The victim's name?
Empathy.

Cause of death?
Murder.
Or neglect.

Either way:
victim suffered
a slow, painful
end,

because we,
the people,
let it happen,

merely watching as
the life left its eyes
and as it gasped
for its last breaths.

Time of death?
The very first moment
that Self-Interest
and Othering were
determined to be laws
of human nature,
rather than flaws
of human thought,

as well as every moment since
in which Humanity
had abandoned
Common Decency,
stabbed Trust
in its back,
and silenced
the voice of Love
in favor of
Ignorance
and Hatred.

So I guess Empathy
and all its friends
are dead.

But this autopsy
is not final.

There is a chance
that Empathy
may still revive.

It just depends
on how many of us
want to see it thriving
again.

By: Joe Z

The Graveyard Locks

Catching wind twisting through the graveyard
With tangled autumn leaves
I slice with scissors moving onward
Quite sure it's not a dream
Protect the violent candle flame
Journey through the maze
The pointed shoulders of your frame
Draw the attention of my gayze
You smile a lipstick-laden smile
And squint under a salute
Despite the sun I'll stay a while
And listen to your fairy flute
The branches recede from the path
Leaving this shy stranger alone
With your haunting hair, a swath
Licking the wind above the worm-thrones
Though short like a soldier's stubble
On the sides of your dryad head
Birds nest it among the rubble
In this sylvan city of dead

1

The Cosmic Witch on Boulevard 66
In a mystic nook of LA malaise
Where semi-corporeal boots tread
Somehow, shrouded less on rainy days
This condo, a shade darker than dread
Though hidden, made clandestine by the sun
To a few it stands out stark and inky
Like a black piano key made ten thousand tons
With a ghastly cat outside a-blinking
Three friends enter through the garden trellis
Giving the cat a light pat on the head
And reach the porch that makes devils jealous
With an entry lamp that's palm-fire red
The bottom floor houses little brick shops
With nary a light on in the windows
And alien murals as a backdrop
Too dim for a phone flashlight inside, though
They take a spiral stairwell up above
With electric cobwebs on the railing
And the final floor houses roosting doves
While the skylight moon casts rays of paling

An incapacious corridor stretches
To a mystic travel agency sign
Its office window graphic glow fetches
Their attention with its neon design
Their tickets ready; their host cracks the door
And with a vinyl hand, beckons them in
To the smell of rocket fuel and much more—
The arcane shape above, of rat fink fins

2

But not two on a classic car, they spied
Three on a rooftop rocket, aiming west
Black as frostbitten chrome—the witch's ride.
She stood beneath a ladder, greeting guests
As we climbed, akin to an attic hatch
Into the pressurized passenger deck
Eye contact lingered before we dispatched
Between she and I during baggage check
They took their seats, the dozen folks or so
Along with my friends in their sable clothes
But the witch asked me if I'd like to know
What it's like up front; I said I suppose
Though on the way to her goth, kitsch cockpit
My slight reluctance was only shyness
Seated beside her at the head of the rocket
Bombarded by her placid slyness
Before I could utter a single word
She pushed the throttle—left the smog below.
We cut through space like a transmundane bird
How far we traveled—did she even know?
The heavens sailed by us like silver streaks;
Planets zoomed in first-person pinball.
As purple Saturn passed she kissed my cheek—
Stars passed like horizontal rainfall
Where we emerged was not the Pearly Way
The speckled void felt strange beyond the glass
But she brushed my hair that had danced astray
On autopilot as the thrusters flashed
Our first destination was a swamp world
An occultist lived there in their condo
With a 3-ringed astro-staff they unfurled
A singing, goblin tulip with a bow

3

We stopped at other planets large and small
I saw industrial, smoke-belching domes
And forests with trees twenty Redwoods tall
Until we arrived at her other home
It was on what I recognized as earth
In a valley northeast of the city
No oranges though, near my town of birth
She lived here, with another black kitty
My friends winked and smiled two suggestive smiles
While awestruck at this different LA
"We—and she—think you should linger a while.
We're going to explore; why don't you stay?"
They said before walking toward the dusk
The fresh electric street lamps guiding them
In the wake of their alchemical musk
Like pilgrims in uncanny Bethlehem
The witch opened her eerie cottage door
A kitsch kaleidoscope on the inside
Her lovely shadow stretched across the floor
An expressionist frame of six foot five
We sat there in her diner-style kitchen
Linoleum decked with arcane symbols
Her attire from burlesque-esque religion
Then with an imperceptible cymbal
She summoned a cup of coffee for me
In a mug I recognized from a dream
With a cute picture of myself and she
Over the words Route 66, it seemed.

4

Autumn Road Abode

The only companions on the lonely autumn road
Dead leaves beyond the windshield, under scorching metal
Dry like the bruised heart's temporary temple
Gently cracked and cradled—delivered to a new abode.

5

The Queendom of Candy-dead
You sit atop a sugar-coated spider
Shimmering in the sunlight
Legs stretch between icing-encrusted castles

Surveying a graham cracker tombstone necropolis
Under a copse of gumdrop mushrooms
The forest reflects its orange and black
Gelatinous shapes in your silver crown
Where they twist and sway like ample dancers
Shaping the powdery, cookie crust path toward
Your victims, tied to pine-sized pretzel sticks
You bundle them in cocoons of cotton candy
With the eight, icepick-sharp legs
Of your spider, whose vile, sweet venom syringes
Turn the downcast faces blue, making
New candy mushrooms among the tombstones
They spill from each gelatinous sarcophagus
A flood of ripe, necrotic fruit cocktail
Tart and red like Tulare cherries
Turning the forest floor to boggy sludge
Now, you swing down between the castles
On a barbed rope of wicked silk
Racing the crawl of sunset shadow
To the place where I hang, atop a cake
From a candy cane candelabra
She takes me by my downward chin
Jabbing with a gentle claw
To meet her octuple-irised eyes
And asks with odd, inklike lips to
Speak the rhyme(s)? with her again:

6

"Kiss me on the cheek—sick as key Lyme cheesecake

Kiss me on the jelly of my eyes
Kiss me as your Queendom's sacrifice
Kiss me in the fading light of day
Kiss my candied flesh to creme brulee"

7

American Gangrene
Haunted every day by the green
Piles of putrid, sterile paper
Is it all the world remains
Capital and cuts, an endless caper?
Is that the rustling of the trees?
Or the billowing bills of debt?
It's the price of life we cannot flee

That ropes a ransom round our necks
On every road we drag our feet
And every blinking sign we see
There's extracted profit so discreet
Our silent shackles scrape the streets
Is there a market for healing?
Unlearning meritocratic means?
Can a Capitalist make it appealing
And gleam on liquid crystal screens?

8

Aroo Aree (A Name Whispered in a Dream of the End)

Aroo Aree
I dreamed of thee
Apocalypse pegasus
Your trail
A tail of wormwood smoke
Choked the life from we
Skating on melting ice
We traced your rotted
Plum reflection
And violet lightning;
It carved a violent slice

9

From Bed to Bed
She was still alive there
But barely

I dragged her from bed to bed
Which were occupied
With other dead
She curled up on the carpet

Let a pet
Resting her white grandma
Dandelion mane

Where the tombstone penned her name

10

Alone with the Lamp

In a dream everything was dark
Someone turned out the moon
I walked from room to room
Following the trickle of liquid
Awakened to the fluidic glare of your hair;
The new home for the moonlight
You wrung the light into a colossal bottle
A lamp to guide me through the trance
Sunk back into sleep, startled
By how dark they were, the neighborhood halls
By touch, explored the doors
Feeling for the familiar engravings;
They opened each porthole, gaping,
Blinking, spheres ringed in eyeshadow
Making muddy, black streams down the stairs
That fill the rooms into dysphoric fish tanks
Where I swim by the bottle-light to the windows

Asleep for far too long
Another night alone with the lamp
You gave me for the maudlin fog
Luminescence from the waking world
That I hope remains on

11

Snaking Coastal Crossroad

Escaping heaven on a snaking coastal crossroad
Rushing through earliest morning mist
Claws of creeping oppressive episodes
Reap asphalt and rain as they persist
Feet float across the tainted waves
Harrowing the endless yarrow horizons
He threads the rope, my millstone grave
Yet this witch, she floats and frightens

12

Altar Sparks (January 7th, 2025)
Trees dance and candles dark
Branches scratch the moonlit sky
Writhing closer, they're torn apart
Venus appears a piercing eye
Karlsvognen, she looms above
Olympian arcs bolt above winter fire

Wood creaks more than enough
To rip the strings from nature's lyre
You fade from sight as smoke blankets
I hail a spell through trees and wires
The golden glitters in thrift store trinkets
And beyond—eerie effulgence of wildfyres

13

Icy Sentinel (a Haiku)
Wintertime Crescent
White as an angel's carcass
Casts shadows through snowy woods

14

The Pale Cherub
Little child—bones and fangs
With a stone between your teeth
Did it quench your hunger pangs
The tomb of shackles underneath?
Or were their superstitions wrong
With misplaced, puritanic pain?
Regardless of the scratches from
You nails upon the window pane
Were you gentle in your gait
By moonlit fields of heather?
And patient in your slumber state
Ere soothing winter solstice weather?
Whether monster—yea or nay
Your sepulcher is a tragic tale
Because when they buried you away
Like anyone, we heard you wail

15

Christmas Paralysis
I awoke to gnashing
And pulled the yellow bedding
Up to the bridge of my nose;
I must have imagined the scratching
I sunk back asleep
And felt constricting fingers
Turn me into a Christmas tree topper
An angel draped in sweaty sheets
My feet dangled darkly

Above the musty mattress
My head in the metal mildew vent
With phantom hands strangling starkly

In the haunted attic
The metal maze was winter
Reflecting fears of years yet unknown
Chromatic bulbs of cosmic static

16

Disremembered December
A sleigh crashed through a tomb
It neglected the ghastly the passengers
Blind to bones from a catacomb's womb
Strewn about by bricks exhumed
They screamed as dead ducts drizzled tears
Wet and wassailing ectoplasm
Missing mistletoe and holiday affairs
A grandmother mourns her phantasm

17

A Quarantine Carol
An incandescent violent
Shining darkly in the bright
Stoops sadly in the quiet
Alone another night
The flower has gone brittle
Forever worse for wear
Things will sting more than a little
Until her loves are near

18

A Sable Shyness
~

Cold and monochrome
Lace and flirty lashes
The shyly trimmed, starless slashes
Fleeing fascist chromosomes

~

19

Shudder & Lens
You hang me from electric chords
For shuttered eyes to see
While magic arrows pierce the words
On pixelated screens
Such fragile normativity
That snips the queerest heartstrings
And leads you to dispose of me
In deleted space, a useless thing

20

Girl Beneath the Lemon Tree
Girl beneath the lemon tree
Alone on bladed soil
The clouds that only she could see
Float low above the leafy veil
Her mild, chameleonic mist
Infected all the glass-eyed playthings
And made their gazes full of wist
And gusted plush—their fabric wings

21

Castle of Atomic Hexes
I wake up in the canopy bed
In this old castle room
I take the silk cap from my head
And place it where I read from
The dusty tomes of my dear father
No dust when I last saw them
Stranger still, no sign of another
Or memories of the times when
I'd see the stained glass in the morning
On the mossy church below
Then leave the lilacs in the graveyard
With sanguine spells of sorrow
Now my dress drags on cobblestone
No souls on either roadside
I knock on the doors of hushed homes
Now no one left to reside
The reticent sounds of songbirds
Invisible to my ears
Alone in this bleak courtyard

This budding garden of fear
My slippers pad the city streets
Skin snowy as the stones
I pray to wake under the sheets
In cloudy memories of home
I reach the town's entrance, ajar
Like a broken cupboard door
I can see them now, not so far
Like broken dolls upon the floor

22

Now their familiar faces
Like beclouded, flexile wax
Shine with sickening glazes
And rosy blisters ringed in black
I stumble, bewildered, backward
Past the crooked portcullis
And crash through a cloud of black birds
Holding in a scream as shrill as
The silence of my late people
No shrieks from my gentle touch
Despite the way their skins sizzle
And to their closest kin, clutch
The empty echo of my sobs
Pull me up these city streets
To the often-rotated knob
Of the room with nostalgic sheets
The sheets under my sleeping-dome
Where I curl up at night
In this draped and canopied room
Rimmed in pulsing, pearly lights
There's a crack in the glassy sheen
Of the clear keeper bubble
That's leaking air of gamma-green
In this room, now mostly rubble
Debris I only notice now
Lies littered about the floor
Among my trinkets and my dolls;
How did I miss it before?
It's so hauntingly obvious
Why there is that glowing green
This deadly plague, notorious
It originates from me

23

I return now, to my tower
Noticing the shriveled flowers
Noticing the weathered vines
In this dead town, only mine

A bird fell from the sky today
After many years have passed
Clutching a scroll from far away
About my castle of the last
They fear me as some toxic witch
Who casts atomic hexes
Who scorched my people in a ditch
And who the visitor vexes
I've been in this place for so long,
That buildings turned to stone from steel
Below this palace, away from
Me—in bedtime tales—real
I hear them on the radio
That my mutant raven stole
Warning children of me, although
The truth of it, they hardly know
No bogeywoman metaphor
For an Iron Age reactor;
I am as real as the acid rain
And composted ancestors
Yet still, I provide the power
For their electric buggies
And kaleidoscopic flowers
From the ruins of my old tower

24

My hair in tight, voltaic curls
Like cyclones in a lightning storm
Attached to sky-cables, unfurled
My swing dress spun in arcane form

Now I'm as old as the great beasts
Whos' feathered bodies turned to tar
Now the world has burned around me

And I can always see the stars

25
Shards of Dysphoric Reflection

Whether the black fabric billows or binds
It cannot unbind the displaced mind
And does little to dim the glimmer
In the tall mirror that shimmers
On the sordid floral stand
Where I simply
Am

Assigned threat at birth, struck soft by command
Too alive to be numb, too glum to be alive
I take the glove from my pallid hand
And run nails like stygian knives
Down the deepening scratches
While keeping candles lit
With dwindling
Matches

26

The Clandestine Carousel

He'll take the children to a pinstriped hell
And lure them with mares of tarnished resin
Tonight, on The Clandestine Carousel

The gramophone groans its musical spell
Numbing the spinning, centrifugal session
He'll take the children to a pinstriped hell

Each pony impaled on a Tesla Coil
Twitching steeds, an electric legion
Tonight, on The Clandestine Carousel

Behind brittle park trees, callous and cold
Rusty gears grind in the winter season
He'll take your children to a pinstriped hell

Under a baleful moon, a cold, mechanical skull
Bares a grim, boundless grin
Tonight, on The Clandestine Carousel

27

For the sake of all madness, theatrical
The mechanized, infernal, Carnival Artisan
Craves keening for his pinstriped hell
Tonight, on The Clandestine Carousel

28

The Sentimental Tiers
Help peel the bricks back
To someplace else—fairytale fantastic
Where nostalgic scents, they never lack
And garden plants are purple plastic
Make the doorways wax and wane
And deadbolts twist to licorice, black
Crack the sugared window panes
And break the blinds to homesick plaque

29

Ageless After Autumn
When I die

Carry Me Down the Stone Steps
To the river where I'll lie
After the Autumn season's left
Lay me in the water
Beneath the deepest palace
Save my seeping soul for later
Under aurora borealis
Every hundred years
Light a candle near my face
Your lips as blue and queer
As mine, under the ice

30

Starving Skin
Starving Skin
Purity Culture, cold and raging
Distant cordial kin
Passive social war waging
To keep us sterile, static
Friendless foes
Pensive, verboten, paralytic

Desperate, overcome with woe

31

The Sterile Steps of Heaven
Descending the sterile, ivory steps
Back to the pre-afterlife for a while
Careful feet flee from heavenly lairs
Of men in white, oil-veined and vile
Their eyes are dingy, pitch things
Still eclipsing, doleful daydreams
Stinging, reflective nether-wings
Spray-tan skin like mildew leather cream

32

Wonder of the Worm
Catharsis of the cobweb
Wonder of the worm
Frail against the coffin-bed
Pale against the earth
Urn of feline at our head
Lover on my left
Will we rise up from the dead?
Or be Grave's ever-guest?

33

Bathtism
Fill my bath
With billionaire blood
To the brim with wrath
Until it's understood
They've siphoned life
From you, us, and me
A wage-slave sacrifice
In the land of the free
They've built an altar
Their christ-linen gangrene
Overflowing, sickly coffers
Heaven's gold, forever obscene

34

A Summer Spider
At night's warm noon

The new and familiar muse
I walked to synthetic soundtracks
Wandering off the world's abuse
Through the town of trees
Out late all lonesome
A dwindled refuge from disease
I felt summer-silk's tickle, wholesome

35

Fire, Fir, and Feline (Geminid Meteor Shower, Full moon, Friday the 13th 2024)

Freya, Witch of Winter's Fire
Of beauty, balsam, fir, and feline
Grasp tightly our doom and desire
As the ever-fading sun declines
Valkyries, with meteor's might
Clash against Midgard's breath
Streaking stars on the 13th night
And a cat-lead chariot's flight
Across the full moon's breadth
Brings her amber dawn of love and death
Hail! Freya, your arnica for anguish
In Winter's fading light

Hail! The Amber Lady shall never languish
Loving embers stoke the fight
Hail! Fire Jewel Freya

With this flame, the gloom we'll vanquish

36

Mothers of Dusk and Dawn (Full Moon, December 2024)
Two goddesses across ancestral seas
Of beauty, love, rebirth, and death

Chosen mothers' hands, reaching through smoke for me
Crow and falcon on a cauldron, singing amber breath

Breaking the lifelong skin-spell
And the final clutch of christened claws
Balm for a baptized child—infused with hell
Comfort from the pads of a cat's cold paws

37

Future Flame (January 7th, 2025)

Candle Glow
How long the dark will last
Only you can know
Fire flows
Although the hills are flame
The worst is yet to show

***

(January 25th, 2025)
Candle glass
The flames are nearly past
New seeds can finally sow
Fading fast
Though hope is fragile still
Let us pray the rain will last

38

The Frozen River
Upon a river of frozen night mares
Ice sprouts from the horses' mouths
With thriving eyes that fear the snare
They crack to life and gallop south
Stiff manes jagged in the hellish cold
Where sepulchrous dreams unfurl
Specter on the event horizon folds
Tempest of haunted hemoglobin swirls
Riding past capillaric passageways
Trampling roses and reaper's dust
They flee the drip from light of day
The red of death and horseshoe rust

39

The Cold Knife of Health
The cold knife of health
Slicing through the fade
Skin hard—heart soft as breath
To dull the icy blade

40

Starlost Lovers
Hello, lover from the stars
You cannot hear me underneath
Your glassy sleep in the astro-car—
A lidded gaze I'll never leave
Copper locks cascade
Across the badge of your jumpsuit
With my nail I'd trace your name
Before our fate turned absolute
A malfunction in my cryobed
Awoke to silence and starry windows
Like candle-specks of the dead
Dim chorus of wraiths crescendo
Nothing I can do
So glad that we did meet
Now out of rationed food
My skeleton soars at your feet

41

Live-in Closet
A day of vitamin D, only
Through the blackout curtain cracks
And scorching blue screens, lonely
While the rainbow keyboard clacks
Until the upside down dawn
Makes a silhouette of light
Melting the dew on landlord's lawn
Ending another lonely night

42

The Hollow Body
A disease between the words
You mimic with your tongues
Bitter rot clings to taste buds
On the way out from your lungs
Many shoulders missing hands
We're Comphet out of fear
You brand your brain with scripture
But for the poor, flow not a tear

43

Barrow of Roses
Inhaled by a grave white roses
Their thorns tear at my skin
Red on white does juxtapose
And color worms that writhe within
Petals caress my viscous wounds
Like paper stuck to cherry jam
My marrow thanks the many boons
Community comfort where I'm damned

44

Sweethaunt
Please linger next time
Hair like streaks of silver
In an oaken night sky
Your phantom outline makes me quiver
Thudding heart rate starts to climb
Still droplets of Summer sweat
From your breasts onto mine
Love made with fresh tears
Drifting down like arson ash
From the flames... an ever-creeping threat

45

The Silver Trainyard
Meet me in the silver trainyard
Made chrome by the mist and rain
The bats above fly quiet and large
With love and melody they shriek you name
The cable cars pass and none ride within
The crack of wings dance through the air
We twirl between the lampost shadows
The station's gleam in the green of your hair

46

Phantasmal Feline
There's a white cat dancing
With six hundred 66 lives
On a headstone prancing
Macabre feline of the flies
Meowing mouth of predator

Soft and super creepy
For her there's no competitor
At being rather eepy

47

A Shadow Above the Cupboard
On an evening when the tape turned to static
Two yellow dots materialized near the attic
By the pull-cord door, latched under ladder
As frozen as I, while the night birds chattered
The cupboard near the hatch—wood and glass
An heirloom from a different time and class
As I slowly blinked it began to rattle
As if the plates and silverware battled
My heart thudded slow despite the panic
That in my dull skull dancing so frantic
Until moonlight hit fur like cotton storm clouds
A comfort for a moment, that translucent shroud
Though not long before a flowing face I cried—
It had been barely a year... since that kitty died

48

The Southernmost Sky
The Southern Star
Led her to the mirrored nether
She sailed without
Compass or earthly tether
The boiling waves
Churned black ice and siren hymns

A blasting gasp
Spat forth the bones of Seraphim
The underworld sky
Its silver eye left maker bare
She shunned him
A patriarch in heaven's lair
Jealous edicts he dreamed of
Ensanguined summons
Vision of crimson communion cups
And scorn for covens
With twisted saintly face, beckoned her
"Neglect your stubborn raft.
Remove abating skin and graft
My old creation—manhood's might

Obey. Abandon femininity's fight
"Fuck you," she breathed.
"I've been further below
My carcass wreathed in angel bones
A sordid sky away, my tombstone."
Her raft ran ashore and abaft was light
Like rain cloud rays, yellow glass stalactites
Too dead to fly, to driven to die swimming
She claimed a piece, steel-keen, grinning

49

"I'm too scarred to feel your lightning-bite!
I'll fight this hellish heaven, finite."

Titanlight
Through the pulp of 1959
She saw a methane ocean
Its alkane spray freckled the dome
Where cosmonauts had made their home

She pressed her face upon the page
Felt the frosty outpost glass
Knew starlight was too distant a kiss
So on Titan's light she'd make her wish

50

Haven in a Haystack
The undying wurm
That roars
In the velvet night
Dwelling in the dim
In the fog where
The streetlight struggles
The night thinks
It knows her well
To neglect her gaze
Would be a crime
Haven in a haystack
Of concrete and grime

51

Crown of Stitches

Kiss this Crown of Stitches good night
She lies deathly still and the walls are white
Heart aligned with the machine that beeps

If the beating ceases
Still yours to keep

52

Babbling Blood
Each crawling tear-trickle
Cherished in fear of good death
Not terror of turning grey
Nor the day of fading breath
But the sight of veins
Blue and green rivers wrapped 'round
My skeleton, cords pulled
Tight, by The Washer at the Ford
The fright of purpose to our pain
Or the thrill of... "will I know you again?"
When will our lips part not in vain
If our souls, our will, speak as the wind?
Clinging to consciousness
Conscious of our bodies stress
Still, I want my flesh to be
A dance of decay, the gentle worm's dress

53

Feathers Found

She'll glide below the autumn gloom
An apparition after August
On the narrowing shaft of light
Wandering toward the afterworld like
The last torch among murky stars

54

Market Macabre

No pages left to live for their own sake
Stakes too high but no midnight oil left to give
Each time our guts are tugged—our rents raised
Their talons still tucked away, rent-free, relentlessly
No notebook safe from the shadow of the job

The macabre market's rotting hooks
Joy's infernal thief, profit-margins praised
That slick-as-slime suits would call eternal

55

A Melancholy Cartoon Backdrop
The sparse trees
And cold, pastel blue sky
And the midcentury sci-fi rocks
Make one wonder what lies
Beyond the faux horizon
A two-dimensional tableau
Intangible in any form beyond
The longing to know what's out there
Beyond the Penciler's intentions
Or the volition of the Pencil

56

Beetle on the Pathway

It kicks and squirm as pedestrians pass by
Almost crunching the bright, reflective belly of blue-green
Hands and knees on white-hot sidewalk, offering an outstretched finger
Making contact with the eerie legs that dance at sanctuary
Clings in desperation—the alien-yet-terrestrial claw
Black exoskeleton hugging human flesh

I let down the rain from my eyes, in tandem with untied hair
It was going to die, like all the other summer kin
Ant-covered husks in the sun now

But no emerald soul unheralded by the Phantom Queen
Washing its tears from my skin in the bathroom brook, now
In the patio shade. Wings sputter. On a leaf of brown and jade.

57

Beneath the Opaque Lace
Your imagination rips me open
A passive aggressive prying eye
Long nails leaving indentations that
I dare not even feign a flinch at, lest I
Be painted in monstrous shades
A titan more vertigo than Virgo

Skeleton unable to constrict strictly enough
To not turn from gorgeous to gorgon
A creature crocheted together femininely
Rather than unravel from fetish to fear
I'm the good luck at the end of your arrow
A dead seabird to solve your two stones
Boyfriend trouble and budding Bicuriousity
Jaw throbbing in my cheeks like rigor mortis
Between bouts of musical coping to the beat
Of twitching earworms I can't unconjure
Until you leave through incandescent fog
Not a single sober moment there to haunt you
The stalker forgets but the siren remembers
When she just wants to dance the chasers away

58

The Other in the Mirror
Their flawless skin in a halo of black
Strands of silken wire
Eyes in a foreign, filigreed mirror
Violet, stark, and staring at
These red and salty spheres
Wielding the waxen lantern's glare
Begging through distorted glass
Lest they make haste and disappear
Away from the interstice, frosty to the touch
Of my blue and lonely fingers
On the other side, over here...

*originally published in The Emma Press Anthology of Contemporary Gothic Verse

59

The Garden Shadow
I felt you in each footfall
That crunched the December decay
Outside the greenhouse tent
Your circling shadow almost one
With the night, though fright
Was as absent as the sun
I felt the whisper of your kiss
As the gust of wind bellowed
Past the tent flaps
Sending shivers around my arms
And legs, passing over my breasts

Like the Paps of Danu, making
Even the dead strands of my hair dance

60

The Moths in the Stairwell
Each sunrise there is a new, patient moth
Whose vision meets the mundane eyes
Of office workers heading down
The speckled steps, through a sea of flies

Like a dead leaf

The moth drifts in the growing puddle
Beyond the buzzing yellow bulbs of suburban lights
Where rain peppers the linoleum tunnel landscape

By: Alex Lorenzen

The Slain Women of Juárez

Thousands of them.
countless faces below desert sands
children, all of them
of the flayed Corn God, Xipe Totec
girls' body parts sprouting
out of an exotic garden—
a toe here, a finger there.

Wide-set brown eyes
broken cheekbones
gray cracked lips
tongues, stiff from
desperate screams
frozen in time
mute to tell their stories of
abductions
murders.

Nameless Indigenous faces
bussed into the border
town of Juárez from
the southern lands of Mexico
thousands of miles away from home
women abducted for cheap labor
and sex slavery.

Once loved in verdant jungles
where women and daughters work, own land
these working women are then lured away
their tierras confiscated by land barons
who see women's bodies as profit
nameless assembly-line workers
virgins of the border
dressed in blue factory smocks
fodder of the maquiladoras.

NAFTA's Free Trade
fair game for senators, police chiefs
narco bosses, and international corporates
landless and alone, women traded
consumed like bocadillos at cocktail parties.

Shoe-lace strangulations
necks, snapped like string beans
breaths sucked out by black suited

vampiros in cowboy boots.

"¡Un Milagro! A Miracle!
The Virgin From Juarez Rises From The Dead."
newspapers from Juárez and El Paso
to the north, announce. "With Bloody Hands
She Crawls Out of Her Own Grave."

Another sensational periodical screams
"Young Woman's Unearthly Voice Heard
At the Dump of The Thousand Faces.
Dry Winds of Juárez, A Spirit Voice Weeps."

A border ballad tells the story
"¿Por qué me hacen llorar?
si nunca hice mal"
"Why do they make me cry?
I've done no wrong."

"My bones far away from my home
my spirit cursed to haunt.
never to be remembered
in this god-forsaken desert."
under you, Moon, I'm buried
yet, you come and go as you please.
"Tú te vas de ronda."*
You go on your rounds.

*song ex, "Noche de ronda," Agustin Lara 1935
"The Slain Women of Juarez." Chicana On Fire, Bambaz Press, 2022.

By: Vibiana Aparicio-Chamberlin

Human Bones

Their teeth always survive
They carry the magical stories and tragic endings

Remains – Bracelets
rosarios, notes and their little-
papelitos with contact numbers

Human bones
Something no one should have to see
Real physical elements

Missing
Mourning
Mad
madres in the front lines

a quiet country
a mother wailing
a quiet system
a sister screaming
loud corrupted system, powered
by el gringo

Human DNA disappears under
Fire, Burning holes
with human remains
Pit of fire burning in
the woods, in the caves, the side of the road

immigrants risking their lives for a chance
to survive
people disappearing by the minute with
nowhere to run
light shut down
The miracle of life taken
now your family yearns for answers
Where can you be?

In a deep hole
A ditch or a trench
Did a Good Samaritan give you a proper burial after finding you?
En el desierto calcinado?
Or perhaps you were burned, chopped or exploded
En el infamous sinister pozole mix

Vanished
Flesh, flies, flushed
Skulls, teeth, spines,
Sparkles in their rosaries
Stories in their backpacks

Shoes

A thousand shoes
A thousand rosaries
A thousand bones
A thousand dreams
A thousand souls, a thousand lives,
a thousand families, a thousand hearts!

El Mexicano se escapa de México para salvar su vida
La vida de sus hijos

Pantalón talla 36
Dentadura entera

Retrieved bodies, retrieved dreams, retrieved screams

Mexico is grieving
Mexico is in pain

Don't step on the human remains
You have done your mission, madres buscadoras

We found 6 full bodies and a few others in pieces
Some keys
A full denture

Pieces of their lives
Dancing with the tales of the past

Recently dead
Today is a good day
Today is a cold day

By: Claudia Ramirez Flores

Reclamation

It's 2025, and all across every single state,
this administration has unleashed its blatant racism and hate.

Not a single person is safe under this appalling regime
in which the breaking of our constitutional rights conveniently goes unseen.

But we will not be held hostage in the land of milk and honey.
No one is above the law, despite their "so-called" money.

God bless every single resident; the red, the white, and the blue.
We, the people, make America great. Trump? Hell no! Not you!

By: Diosa Xochiquetzalcóatl

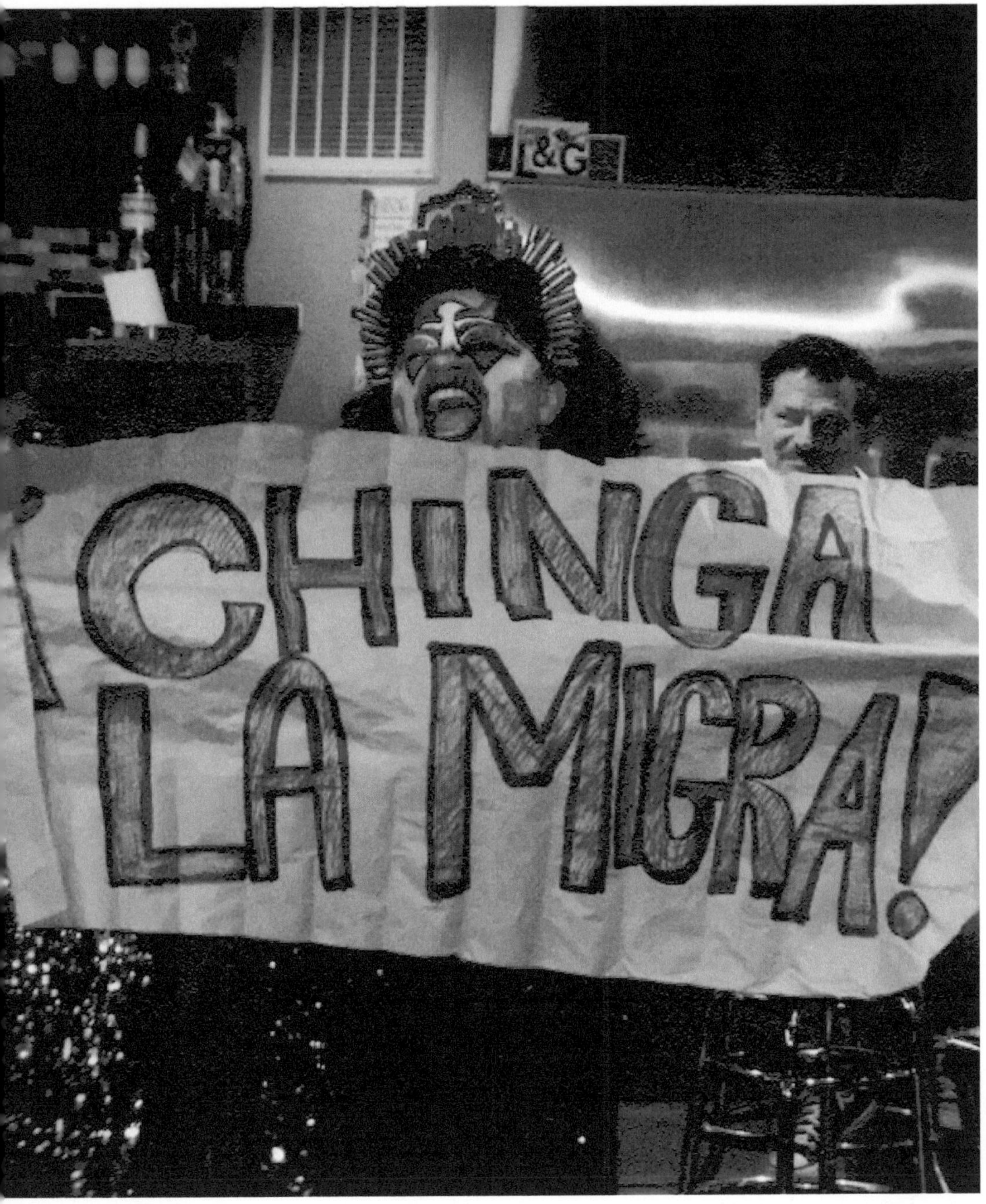

Chinga la Migra;
Executive Suite
King of Drag Show

I stand with women

holding signs of justice
when their rights are at war.
I pray with women
when their children
are taken– enslaved in cages.
I cry with women
when ignorant men
abuse their bodies
        for selfish greed.
I fight with women
against the broken system
we call our home.
Notice, I don't use the word
        for.
I don't stand *for* women
I don't pray *for* women
I don't cry *for* women
I don't fight *for* women
because women are Goddesses
        who need no man to
        stand, pray, cry, or fight *for* them.
Women,
        are the brave warriors fighting for peace.
Women,
        are the thundering echoes in our streets.
Women take their trauma
and turn themselves into a weapon
to rise against the toxic inappropriate
injustice led by men.
I cry with maidens.
I pray with mothers.
I fight with crones.
I stand with women.

By: VOTH

I Don't Want to Be Mexican Today

I don't want to be Mexican today
I don't feel like being Mexican today
I have nothing Mexican to say today

They wait for a song to exit my lips
For me to play a guitar
They wait for me to dance
Or to take a shot of tequila that burns my throat

They sit close to me, but not too close
They want to be friends with me, but not best friends
They invite me, but secretly hope I do not show up

I am sick of softening their stereotypes and prejudices
I am tired of ignoring their racist and hateful speech
          and the lies they spew about me
I am exhausted of being a victim of their discrimination

I will not fake a smile

And I don't feel like being Mexican

I don't want to see myself on Breaking News
or read about me in the newspaper today
I don't want to be racially profiled
or harassed on the streets today
I don't want to have a knee on my back or on my neck
I don't want to be baton whipped today
Or to have ten tons of brick shoved up my ass

Don't ask me to be a Mexican today
I don't feel like being Mexican.

I have nothing Mexican to say.

By: Donato Martinez

La Cobarde Valiente

Sí, yo soy la cobarde valiente que ha luchado con uñas y dientes para defenderse en este país. Como inmigrante siempre seremos discriminados e invisibles para algunas personas especialmente güeros y también latinos porque cuando ya hablan inglés y tienen papeles ellos mismos discriminan con sus propios paisanos.

Acá, si no tienes papeles o no hablas inglés eres una persona invisible y te cuesta mucho poder trabajar y más si trabajas para un negocio americano. Es más discriminación. Te fuerzan a hacer los trabajos más sucios y pesados.

Bueno, yo nunca morí de hambre porque siempre hice la lucha de tener mi dinero, cuidando niños, siempre tenía mis ahorritos. Algunas veces les planchaba la ropa a los muchachos que vivían con nosotros y me daban algo de dinero. Siempre fui luchadora y ahorrativa como mi mamá. Aprendí que siempre debería tener un guardadito para una emergencia. Pero, lo mejor fue cuando empecé a trabajar en una tienda de americanos. Fue mi mayor lucha. "Ralphs," ese fue el nombre de la tienda donde pase los más difíciles retos y racismo. Conocí de cerca lo que era la discrimincación. Y el no hablar inglés fue una gran barrera donde te sientes tan pequeñito o invisible y días y noches de lágrimas y querer renunciar y correr pero la necesidad te detienen. Aguantas hasta más no poder. Pierdes tu autoestima y las ganas de continuar pero también esconderte de los clientes que te quieren preguntar algo y no entenderles porque no hablas ni entiendes el idioma, pero al llegar a la casa y ver a tus hijas emocionadas de tu llegada y abrazarte. Eso es lo que te motiva a seguir adelante. Cuantas veces estuve a punto de tirar la toalla, y salir de ahí, pero el amor de mis hijas me impulsaba a seguir y defenderse y pelear con uñas y dientes. Y llegó el momento.

Y sí llegó mi momento de defenderse y pelear. Saque a la Gina VALIENTE y deje atrás a la cobarde. Como pude hable con el director que no hablaba español, pero alguien me interpretó y di rienda suelta a mis quejas del abuso al que era sometida. Por lo cual llevaron a la manager con la cual yo trabajaba en la noche, la cual me hacía estaquear verdura, poner leche, cerveza, hielo, recoger carros, lavar la carnicería, empacar y hacer gobacks. Los otros trabajadores sólo porque eran güeros cotorreando con la manager y se burlaban. Todo eso le hice saber al director y él habló con Desiree, mi manager y le preguntaron qué por qué. No supo qué decir, sólo se puso roja y se le salieron unas cuantas lágrimas.

Pero desde ese día mi vida empezó a cambiar. Me redujeron un poco el trabajo y cuando le preguntaba a la manager que hacía me decía, "no lo sé." Tenía mucho coraje. Poco a poco empezó a cambiar conmigo. Se volvió más comprensiva y creo hasta se encariño conmigo y me cuidaba.

También, personalmente o individualmente el trabajar me ayudó como ser humano y mujer porque me empecé a sentir liberada, independiente y segura de mi misma por tener mi propio dinero y no depender de nadie y darme cuenta que si era y soy muy VALIENTE. Deje atrás a la COBARDE.

By: Gina La Valiente

The Brave Coward

I.

Yes, I am the brave coward who has fought tooth and nail to defend herself in this country. As an immigrant we will always be discriminated against and invisible to some people especially light-skinned people and also Latinos because when they already speak English and have papers they themselves discriminate against their own countrymen.

Here, if you don't have papers or you don't speak English you are an invisible person and it is very hard for you to be able to work and even more so if you work for an American business. It's more discrimination. They force you to do the dirtiest and heaviest jobs.

Well, I never starved because I always fought to have my money, babysitting children, I always had my little savings. Sometimes I ironed the clothes for the young men who lived with us and they gave me some money. I was always a fighter and thrifty like my mother. I learned that I should always have a little saved for an emergency. But, the best was when I started working at an American store. It was my greatest struggle. "Ralphs," that was the name of the store where I went through the most difficult challenges and racism. I got to know up close what discrimination was. Not speaking English was a big barrier where you feel so small or invisible and days and nights of tears and wanting to quit and run away but necessity stops you. You endure until you can't anymore. You lose your self-esteem and the desire to continue but also hide from customers who want to ask you something and you don't understand them because you don't speak or understand the language, but when you get home and see your daughters excited about your arrival and hugging you. THAT is what motivates you to keep going. Many times I was about to throw in the towel, and leave, but the love of my daughters pushed me to continue, defend myself and fight tooth and nail and eventually the moment arrived.

II.

Yes, my moment to defend myself and fight arrived. I brought out Brave Gina and left the coward behind. As best I could I spoke with the director who did not speak Spanish, but someone interpreted for me and I let loose my complaints about the abuse I was subjected to. For which, they brought in the manager who I worked with at night. The one who made me stack produce, put out milk, beer, ice, collect carts, clean the butcher, pack and do go-backs. The other workers, just because they were light-skinned, chatted with the manager and had fun. I made all of that known to the director and he spoke with Desiree, my manager, and asked her why. She did not know what to say, she just turned red and a few tears fell.

From that day forward my life began to change. They reduced my work hours a little and when I asked the manager what I did she would tell me, "I don't know." I was very angry. Little by little she began to change. She became more understanding and I think she even grew fond of me and looked out for me. She also, personally, or individually worked to help me as a human being and woman. I began to feel liberated, independent, and confident in myself by having my own money, and not depending on anyone and realizing that I was and am very BRAVE. I left the COWARD behind.

By: Gina La Valiente

No Good Way

The Apple News notification
pops up on my screen again.

I take a glance, and a single line
immediately catches my eyes:

There's no good way to kill somebody.

This is apparently
said with regard
to the death penalty[(1)]
within the U.S.A.,
and I can't help but agree,

because with each passing day,
it seems as if this place becomes
more and more known for its
decades of homegrown atrocities
committed in the names of
Liberty
and
Justice for All;

because the history of this country
is a white canvas painted
red in blood
and
blue in tears,

a legacy of tainted arts
(like bigotry and war)
unworthy of either praise or cheer.

There's no good way to kill somebody.

These words now echo in my mind
constantly, reminding me
of all the people sentenced to
detention in concentration camps
for simply looking different,
speaking different,
or coming from a different land

often rife with strife,

because many of those
held in detention are
essentially sentenced
to die.[2]

And the refrain replays again in my head:

There's no good way to kill somebody,

not by murder;
not by starvation;
not by torture;
not by incarceration;
not by abduction;
not by infection;
not by poverty;
not by bullets or blades
or bombs or bureaucracy.

There is
no
good
way
to kill.

So why do we still pretend
there is any mercy or justice
in deciding how others' lives
should end?

By: Joe Z

(1) From an Apple News In Conversation podcast episode: https://podscan.fm/podcasts/apple-news-in-conversation/episodes/theres-no-good-way-to-kill-somebody-what-the-death-penalty-looks-like-in-america

(2) Different news outlets and journalists have found this to be true, for example: https://www.newsweek.com/ice-detention-center-migrant-deaths-rising-2093770

Flutes

Juan Flautistas flute
Will never be heard again in L.A.
Some things are hard to say.
When self-deportation is the best choice
Los Angeles screams and starts losing its voice
Drowned in the white noise
So here I am, a ventriloquist
Trying to transmit the mute sound of the immigrants.
I would tell you how to love me, but I doubt you can relate,
Love is such a foreign concept, pun intended,
So I'll take time to show you how
To hate a Latino.
Something you already do.
First we have to understand why there is even hate in you.

To hate a Latino,
You gotta hate yourself.
But never let it show
In fact, show the opposite.
To take the time and energy to go out of your way
And hate, means that you are not content with the life you undertake.

To hate a Latino means he must have done you wrong,
He must have jailed your brother, or deported your mother,
You do not need to love me, I'm not even a Latino.
I'm a Mexican American, whose birthright may be illegal.

I exhale black clouds on a bright sunny day
Dioses Aztecas, deluges in Tejas.
The God Feather serpent
Is crying rivers of Guadalupe.
Is mount Olympus hard to reach,
There is one lesson we should teach.
To love the world despite its ego.
To love regardless if you're legal.

By: Carlos Ornelas

Alex Jeffrey Pretti is Dead.
Minneapolis, MN
January, 24, 2026

The United States of America lost another life to ICE
Alex Jeffrey Pretti is dead
His last words show the man he was
Protecting others in moments that should not have been his last

"Don't touch her!"

Under Minnesota sun he knew well
An outdoorsman
A nurse

His last act
Protection and care
For a woman thrown down

"Are you okay?"

No more hikes under Minnesota skies

No more grace for a government gone awry

By: Cherice Cameron

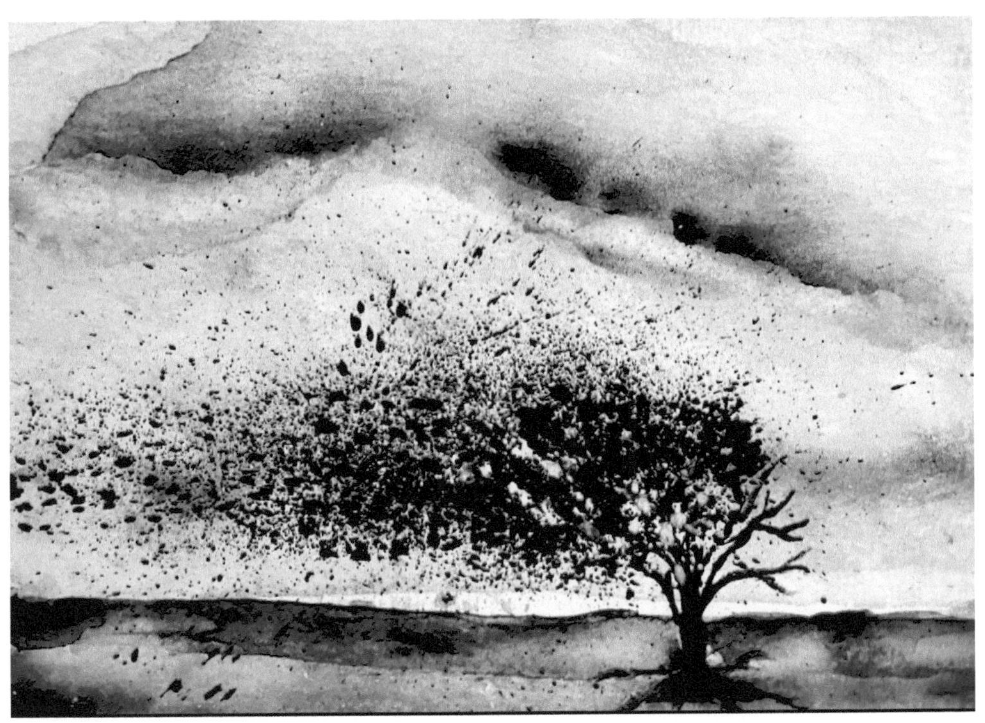

By: Joe Crowley

Don't Forget, Remind Yourself

Looking over my shoulder.
Unmarked cars, masked men,
talks of hay un retén.

White supremacy's at an all time high,
while common sense and critical thinking is low.
But my brown pride doesn't let it consume me.
I know I'm resisting.
I'm an educated brown woman.
Emotionally wealthy, healthy,
Intelligent brown woman.

I've marked my place here
In your so-called America.

Immigrants are the reason America's survived.
You were too busy murdering indigenous people,
drugging them up. Too busy taking land,
knitpicking who's qualified to have rights.
Cuz while your white citizens who don't work are busy fenty-folding,
we're 'taking away' jobs they're too proud to do
or perhaps too lazy.

It's crazy how when we work an honest days work it's 'dirty'
But when you do, it's 'artisan'.
When we cross the border we're just a useless body in America,
but when you do it, it's Manifest Destiny.
When we shop second hand it's because
'we have too many mouths to feed' but
When you do it it's up-cycling.
It's 'trendy', it's 'vintage',
You depop reseller.

I see the news of ICE hitting quotas.
Of Mr Oink banning boycotts in the UC system,
Of that bill...the Big, Beautiful bullshit.
You see, he wants to get rid of the hard workers.
The dads in East LA trying to send his kids to college.
The moms in Sun Valley buying the month's groceries,
her kid that just became an IFEP in first grade.
The brothers and sisters who stopped their commute to work
to hit record.

Only for them to get shoved to the ground,

According to your Constitution we have freedom of speech.
But is that before or after you smash our car window?

This country hasn't felt like it was mine since 2016.
My laments fall upon deaf ears.
President Trump, why don't you hear us?
Are you too busy making out with Jeff Bezos then calling
Zuckerberg in tears explaining how it didn't mean a thing?

Don't forget your wife's an immigrant.
Don't forget your son was born to one too.
Don't forget you're not indigenous.
Remind yourself you're an immigrant too:
Remember your grandpa wanted the American Dream.

Don't forget that we're human.
Don't forget there's a God.
Don't forget that he loves us.
Remind yourself to love thy neighbor.
Remember his name is Juan.

I met a Hispanic Donald.
In fact, he was the hardest working of his crew.
And you know what's funny?
Us Latinos love to name our kids 'America'.
I knew about four in middle school.

Mexican America from Puebla,
Salvadoran America from Usulután,
Cuban America who thought she was the whitest America,
and Dominican America who told her to shut up every time
she called herself güerita cuz
America never lets colorism die.

Don't forget we're resilient.
Don't forget that we're educated.
Don't forget immigrants get the job done.
Remind yourself you're not indigenous.
Remember you're walking on stolen land.
Don't forget your conviction charges.
Don't forget January 6th.
Don't forget that America was already great.
Remind yourself you're a felon.
Remember we will forever remember you are the worst President in history.

By: Katherine Preza Lenore

ESL4L

The old white Storytelling professor singled me out in class,
smugly declaring: *I can tell English was not your first language, right? What was your first language?*

Spanish.

Yes, she nodded with satisfaction, *your accent has almost gone away, but I can still hear it.*
I sat there, dumbfounded that this professor thought it was a good idea to say that to one of her students, in front of the rest of class.

What was I supposed to do? Congratulate her hearing at her age?

Pride won out all of the other emotions that day, in my mind at least.
I wished everyone I came across could hear my struggle to standardize my Inglés in every syllable I spoke. My innate refusal to wash away mi identidad. I also wished I had the language and courage to tell the old lady off. I would have told her:

Soy Mexicana y American
with an emphasis on the Mexican.
Damn right the colonizer's tongue
did not conquer my mouth or mi alma.

My mother's tongue
has allowed it to
vivir en paz, but only
porque nos beneficia.

Hable exclusivamente Español,
for five years before a single word of
English was forced into my mouth in Kindergarten,
lloraba y lloraba porque
no entendia.
it would frustrate me, frighten me
to not be amongst the soft, round, emotive sounds
that belonged to my family. I didn't want to, but I knew I had to
assimilate.
A necessity, because my parents didn't risk their lives coming here for nothing.
Mi papá, a proud citizen of the US, siente gratitud y lealtad to a country que nos quiere sacar. I can't tell him anything about the country that gave him su negocio.

After breaking his back his entire life, he deserves so much more, yo pienso. Él y mi mamá lo dieron todo por nosotros, y yo también lo doy por que se sientan orgullosos.

No one works harder than the children of immigrants.
Before I knew it, I was fluent, and with a lot of work from my 3rd grade teacher who wanted to rid me of the stigmatizing ESL label, I was "reclassified" to EO, to my mom's delight. Tragic

how replacing the "Second Language" next to English with "Only"
is a cause for celebration.

The English Proficiency Exam is racist, I tell my ESL students. They look around, and I watch it sink in. When they repeat it to other students and teachers, I feel like I'm planting seeds to the revolution. I make sure they are proud of their ability to speak two languages fluently. *You know they pay you extra for being bilingual and helping with translations?* I hope they do a better job keeping their Spanish than I have.

I know I should be thankful for being an "anchor baby," but I can't help but think about all that was taken from me by living in duality.
I am still proudly ESL, proclaiming it to anyone who dares make fun at how I pronounce unknown words phonetically.
Spanish sounds don't betray me the way English ones do, the way I betrayed my Mother's tongue.

While Spanish words still manage to flow out of me pretty seamlessly,
there is an undeniable struggle that my parents and family lovingly
make fun of me for. I make up words a lot.

I would have told that professor all of that, and finished with,
I wear the remnants of being ESL like a prize I labored to win and am still laboring to keep. I hope the glue that keeps those parts of mi lenguaje
stuck to my English never wears out. They may have reclassified me to English Only, but yes, bitch, English was my Second Language. I'm re-reclassifying myself.

By: Ely Lupe

Declaración de los ancianos del movimiento por los derechos civiles sobre los derechos humanos y las políticas de inmigración en el orden mundial capitalista/imperialista

1 de junio de 2025

Con el espíritu de defender los intereses de la clase trabajadora y dejar las cosas claras en relación con la política de reforma migratoria en los EE. UU., declaramos el derecho al trabajo libre de intimidación, demonización y / o división como un derecho humano. Desde las luchas contra la esclavitud y el feudalismo, hasta las batallas contra la explotación capitalista y los órdenes mundiales imperialistas, la lucha de clases ha sido la forma más efectiva de exigir respeto, igualdad y justicia social en el mundo.

La historia mundial nos ha enseñado que las poblaciones han migrado dentro y fuera de todos los continentes históricamente, soportando la ira del odio, la división, la explotación y la exclusión basada en sus orígenes nacionales en cada lugar de asentamiento. Las relaciones políticas y económicas con las poblaciones migrantes/inmigrantes, con las políticas gubernamentales con las que se encuentran, se basan en los órdenes económicos controlados por las clases dominantes adineradas que buscan proteger su riqueza a través de la continua división y abuso de esas poblaciones humanas.

Estas son las realidades fundamentales del orden mundial contemporáneo, dirigido por un imperialismo estadounidense que está en un estado de decadencia, similar a los imperios del pasado que abusan de las poblaciones mediante guerras, genocidios, monopolios de recursos y explotación. La historia de Estados Unidos de construcción y desarrollo de estados nacionales está repleta de abusos, genocidios y explotación, que proporcionaron a sus señores esclavistas fundadores la base para el sistema actual del capitalismo, con su sistema de trabajo forzado y explotación de las poblaciones migrantes/inmigrantes como un ejército de reserva de mano de obra.
Los programas expansionistas a través de la acumulación de ganancias de mano de obra esclava, el adelgazamiento genocida de las poblaciones nativas y los programas de expulsión (rastro de lágrimas), y la política del destino manifiesto a través de la doctrina Monroe del siglo XIX cimentaron la ideología nacionalista del "sueño americano". Las expansiones del siglo XIX a través de guerras violentas y la manipulación de las reconfiguraciones eurocoloniales de las divisiones de propiedad y territorio dieron lugar a redistribuciones de la población, conducentes a la solución de "su" problema de esclavos, y a la creación de programas de inmigración e inmigración.
La primera en la historia de Estados Unidos se formuló en 1848 con la firma

del Tratado de Guadalupe Hidalgo entre las fuerzas mexicanas derrotadas que perdieron el 50% de su territorio en ese periodo. Un supuesto compromiso para otorgar la ciudadanía a los mexicanos que vivían en el territorio cedido se negoció bajo la coacción de la guerra y la especulación de que Estados Unidos tendría que manejar a esta "población extranjera" a raíz de las divisiones sobre su sistema esclavista y la captura de esclavos.

De hecho, la dinámica política en ese mismo período condujo a una ley que abordaba el tratamiento de los esclavos fugitivos de manera similar a las redadas actuales de ICE, donde los agentes del gobierno de los EE. UU. pueden arrestar y extraditar a una persona sin orden judicial y/o juicio. El actual estratega legal de la administración estadounidense tomó prestada la "Ley de Esclavos Fugitivos" de la década de 1850 que permitía a los cazadores de esclavos, o a cualquier otro acusador blanco, declarar ante un juez que una persona negra es un fugitivo, y que serían arrestados y extraditados sin una orden judicial o juicio. Nuestras comunidades son los nuevos "esclavos negros fugitivos" a los ojos del gobierno federal, donde cualquiera puede ser acusado de ser una amenaza para el estado nación, barrido en forma calculada de tropas de choque y mantenido cautivo o trasladado a centros de detención sin protecciones legales.

Esta horrible satanización de los trabajadores no es nueva para las poblaciones no europeas en los EE.UU., como lo demuestran los ciclos de políticas y/o leyes racistas del gobierno de los EE.UU. en respuesta a su actual crisis económica y social. Desde las primeras proclamaciones de "exclusión legal" bajo la Ley de Exclusión China en el siglo XIX, hasta la nueva exclusión de los "anarquistas" en el siglo XX durante la Revolución Mexicana, pasando por el Movimiento de Repatriación de la era de la depresión de los años 20-30, el Programa Bracero de la década de 1940, las redadas de la Operación Espalda Mojada de la década de 1950 y las continuas redadas del ciclo de recesión hasta la fecha, nuestra comunidad ha luchado y perseverado contra probabilidades increíbles.

La actual situación política y económica en Estados Unidos, y en el mundo, ha dado lugar a la misma respuesta fea y temerosa de las generaciones pasadas de exclusión racial. La camarilla de la clase dominante que diseña la división en las poblaciones de la clase trabajadora, todo en su plan para proteger el sistema que acumula su riqueza, ha sido desafiada con el declive de su nuevo orden mundial y su miedo a perder el control de los recursos en todo el mundo. La respuesta doméstica típica se basa en precedentes históricos que utilizan la división racial, enfatizando una amenaza a la cultura dominante (es decir, el poder mayoritario euroamericano), la vergüenza de la crisis económica y la extralimitación patriótica o militar.

La lucha por la unidad de la clase trabajadora, basada en el internacionalismo, debe ser el común denominador para activar a la masiva

población en Estados Unidos para bloquear la agenda de odio y los ataques a los sectores más pobres de nuestro país. Nuestras experiencias desde la década de 1960 hasta la fecha han dado lugar al cambio, la generación envejecida de oportunistas políticos en las instituciones gubernamentales está trabajando para revertir el cambio, reclutando a una nueva generación de explotadores, traficantes de odio y demagogos desalmados.
Debemos apelar al sentido común, educar a una nueva generación de activistas y facilitar un movimiento estructurado a través de una red de consejos asesores y acciones organizacionales.

By: Miguel Lopez

President of Chicano Moratorium

Declaration of the elders from the civil rights movement regarding human rights and immigrant policies in the capitalist/imperialist world order

June 1, 2025

In the spirit of defending working-class interests, and setting the record straight related to the politics of immigration reform in the U.S., we declare the right to work free of intimidation, demonization and/or division as a human right. From the struggles against slavery & feudalism, to the battles against capitalist exploitation and imperialist world orders, class struggle has been the most effective way of demanding respect, equality, and social justice in the world.

World history has taught us that populations have migrated in and out of every continent historically, endured the wrath of hatred, division, exploitation, and, exclusion based on their national origins in each location of settlement. The political and economic relations with migrant/immigrant populations with the government policies of which they encounter, are based on the economic orders controlled by wealthy ruling classes that seek to protect their wealth through continued division and abuse of those human populations.

These are the fundamental realities of the contemporary world order, led by a U.S. Imperialism that is in a state of decline, similar to the empires of the past that abuse populations through wars, genocides, resource monopolies, and exploitation. The U.S. history of nation state building and development is replete with abuse, genocide, and exploitation, that provided its founding slave lords the basis for the current system of capitalism, with its system of indentured labor and exploitation of migrant/immigrant populations as a reserve army of labor.

Expansionist programs through slave labor profit accumulation, genocidal thinning of the native populations and removal programs (trail of tears), and, the policy of manifest destiny through the 19th century Monroe doctrine cemented the nationalist ideology of the "American Dream". The 19th century expansions through violent wars, and manipulation of Euro colonial reconfigurations of property/territorial divisions gave rise to population redistributions, conducive to solving "their" slave problem, and, creating migrant/immigration programs.

The first in U.S. history was formulated in 1848 with the signing of the Treaty of Guadalupe Hidalgo between the defeated Mexican forces losing 50% of their territory in that period. A supposed compromise to grant citizenship to Mexicans living in the ceded territory was negotiated under duress of war, and speculation that the U.S. would have to manage this "foreign population" in the wake of divisions over their slave system, and, capturing slaves.

In fact, the political dynamic in that same period led to a law that addressed the treatment of fugitive slaves similar to the current sweeps by ICE, where the U.S. government agents can arrest & extradite a person without warrant and/or trial. The current U.S. administration's legal strategist borrowed from the 1850s "Fugitive Slave Law" that allowed slave hunters, or any other white accuser, to declare to a judge that a black person is a fugitive, and they would be arrested and extradited without a warrant or trial. Our communities are the new "black slave fugitives" in the eyes of the federal government, where anyone can be accused of being a threat to the nation state, swept up in calculated shock troop fashion, and held captive or removed to detention centers without legal protections.

This horrible demonization of working people is not new to non-Euro populations in the U.S., with proof through cycles of racist U.S. government policies and/or laws in response to their on-going economic and social crisis. From the first "legal exclusion" proclamations under the Chinese Exclusion Act in the 19th century, to the new 20th century exclusion of "anarchist" during the Mexican Revolution, through the 1920-30s depression era Repatriation Movement, the 1940s Bracero Program, the 1950s Operation Wetback raids, and continued recession cycle raids to date, our community has fought back and persevered against incredible odds.

The current political and economic situation in the U.S., and the world, has given rise to that same ugly and fearful response of the past generations of race baiting exclusion. The ruling class cabal that engineer's division in the working-class populations, all in their plan to protect the system which garners their wealth accumulation, has been challenged with the decline of their new world order and their fear of losing control of resources worldwide. The typical domestic response is based on historic precedent utilizing racial division, emphasizing a threat to the dominant culture (i.e. Euro-American majority power), economic crisis shaming, and patriotic or military overreach.

The struggle for working class unity, based on internationalism, must be the common denominator to activate the massive population in the U.S. to block the hate agenda, and the attacks on the poorest sectors of our country. Our experiences from the 1960s to date have given rise to change, the aging generation of political opportunists in government institutions are working to reverse the change, by recruiting a new generation of exploiters, hate mongers, and heartless demagogues.

We must appeal to common sense, educate a new generation of activist, and facilitate a movement with structure through a network of organizational advisory councils and actions. A united front against the new fascism of the billionaire ruling class, POWER TO THE PEOPLE!

By: Miguel Lopez
President of Chicano Moratorium

A Reaction to an Execution

America is ripping out her fingernails
as we speak
America is beating her teeth out
with a hammer
the spotlight is on her
her only performance to bleed for us
she bleeds and bleeds
and tries to rip her hair out to
staunch the bleeding

it doesn't work
it doesn't work–
America has an infection
she walks and spits the fever out of herself
she tramples corn, squash and beans
under her bare rough feet

kind hands offer America
sweet oranges and bright lemons
to ease the thorn in her throat
and the dust in her eyes

America crushed the fruit
with her bloodied fingers
and questions and interrogates
brown hands

the spotlight is on America now
and she protects the weeds
and breaks her knees
ripping out every vine, sprout, and fruit
and letting the seeds wither in the ashes of America's hair

america is slowly killing herself
and all we can do
is beg her to stop

when America finally

rots herself to the ground
we will wait,
For the body to disintegrate
For the sun to bleach the bones
Let forest fires purify the earth
And wait for blessed rain
Those of us remaining after her
Execution will
till the grave and seed the earth softer
praying something better will rise from the corpse.

By: Hope Cerna

Caution:
Mexican Poppy
just not for your
consumption under

the orange sun sliding down
the fretless neck of the
violet sky singing its hymn
to an enharmonic quarter note C

sharp like the sting of birthing
prickly spines on wild poppies
self-preserved with poisonous
sticky yellow alkaloid

sap sinking smoothly
still as the sun stretches
its shining arms towards
earth stained with stories

passed over fences
check-points armed guards
shimmering cars with fumes
more toxic than a small

yellow petalled flower growing
on its native soil extending prickly
leaves intended for
medicine in knowing hands—

just not for your
consumption whistles
the sun's winds flat
as a whole note D

By Gina Rae Duran

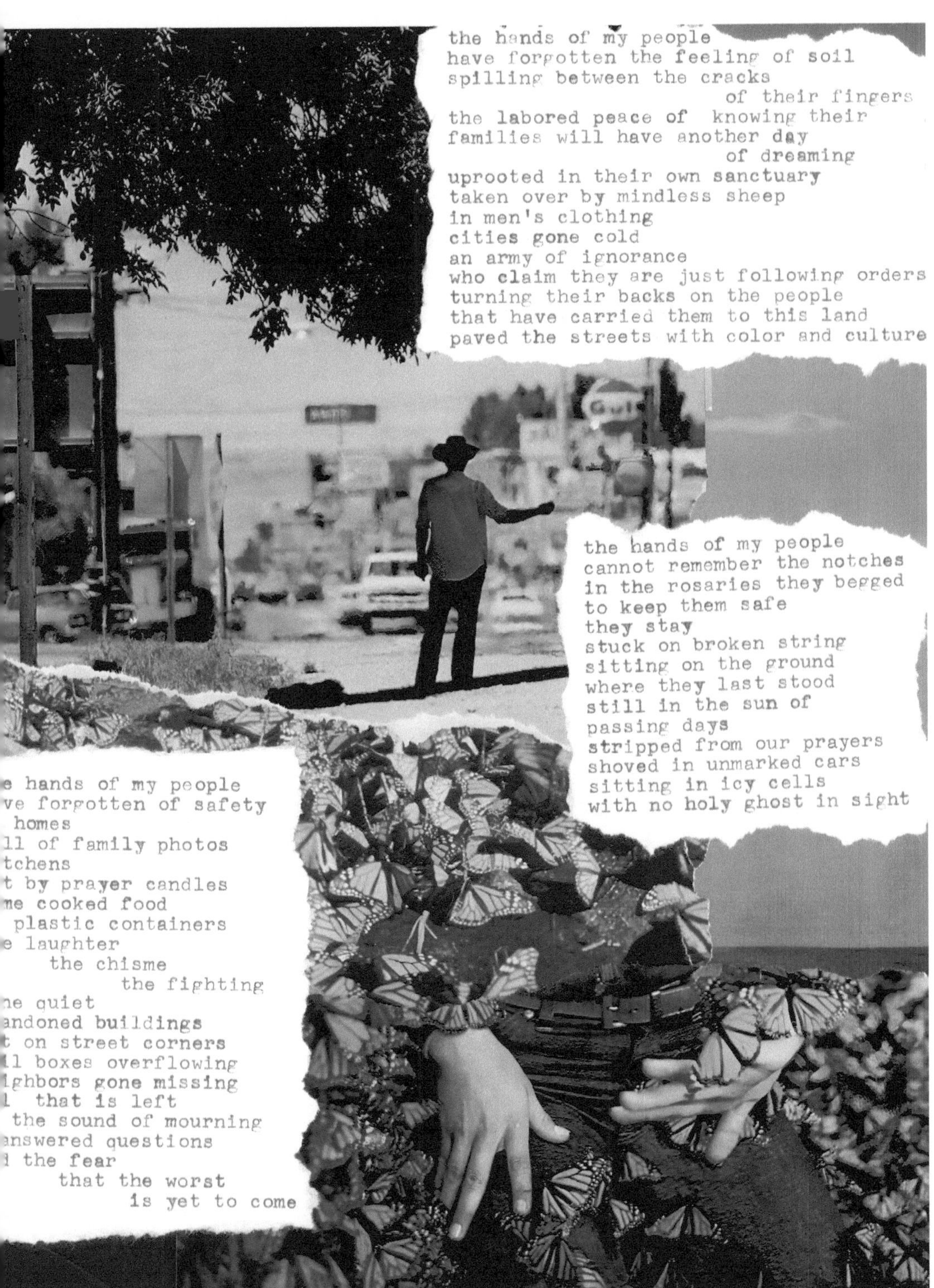

y: Samantha "Sammy" Herrera

You Will Not

You will not take my friends.
You will not take their families.
You will not tell me who to fear.

I walk around in a world of color,
colors I can see,
but refuse to let define
my boarders of interaction.

I eat dinner with friends
at a Korean BBQ restaurant
in Koreatown,
Los Angeles.
A white man,
a black man,
Taiwanese American woman,
a Pilipino American woman,
laughing about past memories,
a drunken graduation night
from grad school, my friend
Kelly nearly throwing up
in my car.

I walk around in a world of color,
colors I can see…

I met a writer, Feroz,
in my Fresno State
MFA program,
who needed a friend
7500 miles from his home
in Kashmir,
his Muslim roots. He writes
about the atrocities of war
he lived through,
the senseless killings of the Indian Army,
a recurrent dream
where “the street is a litter of limbs

and stones and broken glass." We grew close,
pushed each other as writers.

I refuse to let color define
my boarders of interaction.
If I had
I would never have the memories
with my first love,
a Chicana from Inglewood. The night
of my grad night, too tired,
exhausted,
collapsing on my bed,
our eyes shutting tight,
my arm draped snugly
across her torso.

You will not take my friends.
You will not take their families.
You will not tell me who to fear.

I will not succumb to your falsehoods
and lies. "Rapists and drug dealers" I
have never met,
but real people
with a beating heart,
with precious breath,
that speaks truths
I can more closely relate to
than anything you spit from your lips.

I will not
            label them at all.

By: Brian Dunlap

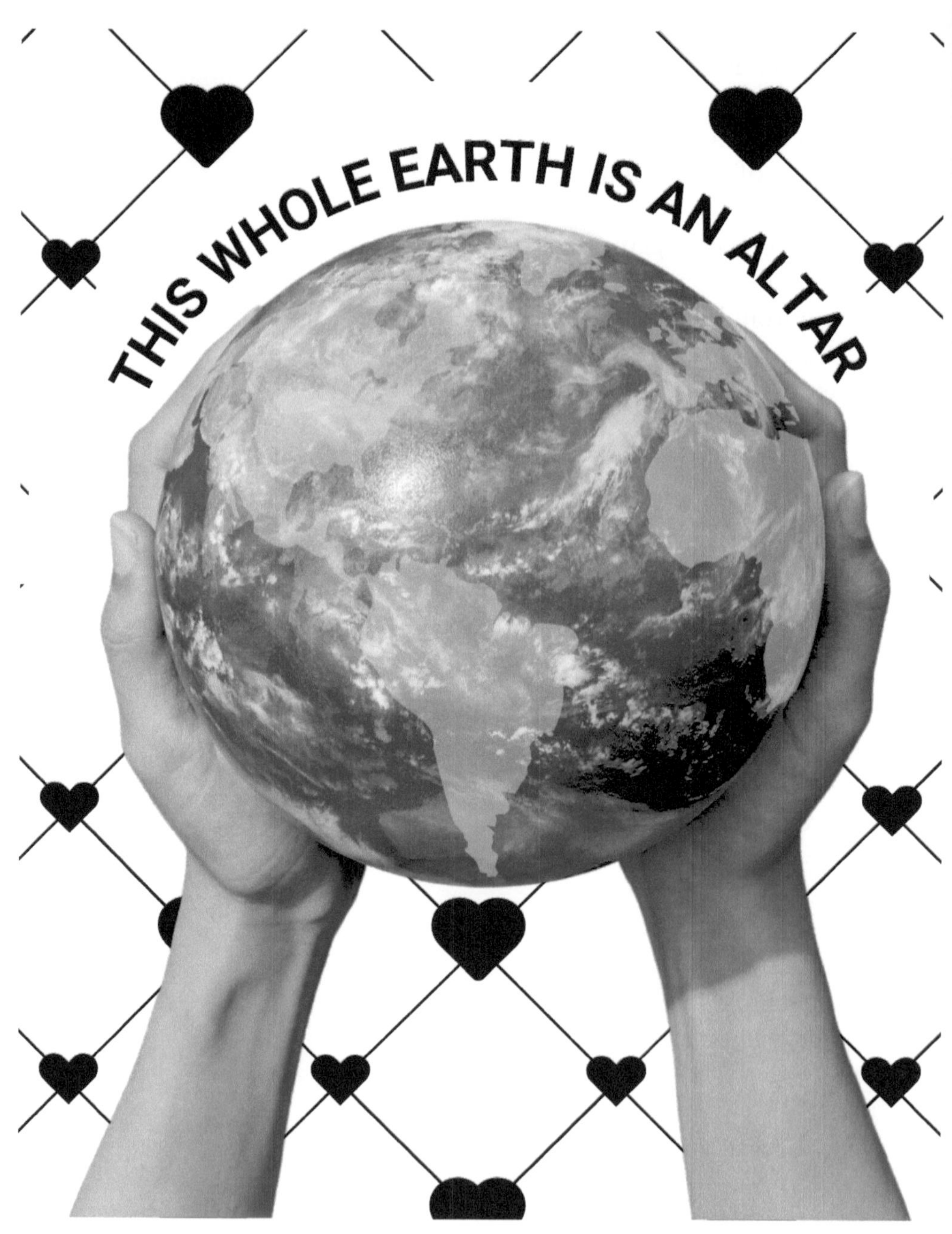

By: Ana Goodman Herrick

Company

This canela
Brown skin of mine carries
A degree of history with a pinch
Of spicy misery as its seasoning
Sprinkled over centuries of my ancestry

You don't believe come get a taste of me
So you can understand why dissent is indigenous
To my inner-fields that yield crops of insurgency

You see
I'm a descendant, a product of war
My melanin carries a legacy
That on hot summer days
It don't hesitate to seep thru my pores

I sweat
Droplet of Mexico's 1910 revolution
I sweat the spirit of Emiliano Zapata
Screaming: I'd rather die fighting on my feet
Than live a lifetime on my knees

In my eyes
Pupils you can see
Pancho Villa riding for the stolen
Land Uncle Sam in 1846
Took from Mexico's hand

My fingertips
The contours on them resemble the field
Where to this day, farmworkers harvest
The crops dropped off at local stores
Yet at the border they closing the doors
I think they forget America be sustained
By immigrants from all over the world
Give'em amnesty, full citizenship, and more!

Yo! But my feet
Never walked it, I never made the journey from
Mexico, Guatemala, Belize, Honduras, El Salvador
I'm a seed of immigrant parents, father from Vera Cruz
Mother from a "pueblo" outside Mexico City, San Mateo Atenco

I happen to sprout out the cracks
Of a ghetto trash-crowded sidewalk
The gutter of a supposed civil society

Which "casi nadie" give a fuck about
Where hardly anyone shines a beam of hope
But I ain't sinking 'cause I'm not on a boat
Despite the legacy of misery
Sprinkled over my ancestry
I stand afire sending signals of smoke

Because my ancestry's history
Contains a universe unexplored
Whose essence can't be captured
By words an author wrote

It contains
Clusters of constellations
Tribal nations living in unification
With each other and the ways of Earth
Knowledge
Known: that harming her is no doubt
Only ourselves we hurt
But I'm
Not ready or willing to
Make a turn for the worst
In my arms I'll carry my culture first
Before I help to carry it
Out of this world in a casket

Like a volcano with pride I'll burst
Burning to ashes the disrespect
The rude and crude attitude shown
My people of the sun
For you I keep a song of hope on my tongue

And in my memory runs
Your revolution prone
Cyclone on a megaphone
Shouting echoes that never let go
Or get tired of reminding me
Of the legacy that my flesh embodies

So when the sun bathes my body
And at an angle you're able to see
My shadow and its following
As for the extra company
They are my ancestry
Which this canela
Brown skin of mine carries

By: Andres RHIPS Rivera @rhips (on all socials)

From the Clouds

We are people of the clouds.
We are from the mountains,
the air and the sun.
My grandfather used to say that
we are tall like the milpa
in our spirits.
This Earth belongs to us.
Our bodies melt into the ground,
sometimes lost and never seen again.
We are drowning in the concrete.
Will our feet ever touch the ground?
I've heard stories about *coyotes,*
about borders,
about the river,
the endless poems uncovered on his *petate.*
Papi closes his eyes and remembers his mother's hands
squeezing him tight.
She turns her fingers into a cross
and holds them up against his lips.
Before she died, the wind gathered him
behind the bushes.
She had forgotten the face that she birthed,
especially his eyes.
She only knew her son through letters.
Through the hearts that left her home hollow.
Each time, the emptiness bloomed.
I remember his *gritos*,
the way they stung me in my chest.
They echoed in the ocean,
across different walls,
between fears and wonders.
"En unos años yo también seré polvo," he says.
"Returning to the land that raised me,
the land that has continued to love me
even though my viejos left it all behind.
This land that is mine.
This land that is mine.
This land that is mine.
this land that I said goodbye to
forever.

By: Clara Ximena Roque-Wagner

show up

the last gasps of afternoon sunlight stream in through the blinds,
they coat my niece
me
and the dolls in our hands
in a layer of molten amber,
and I wonder,

can she hear them?

the question sinks its fangs into my ankles
gnawing away at flesh and bone
as we guide our petite protagonists
through the world we're constructing
here on the floor of Huela's living room

I just want to know
        if she can hear the cracks
        zig-zagging their way
        across my heart,
            the tectonic plates shifting
        beneath the pressure and promise of
            another colonization
        another carnal continent at risk of being consumed
            by a manifest destiny of
            rage,
            ego,
            and
            hatred

Man,
I don't know

homegirl is only 4 years old and
unsurprisingly
out of fucks to give

instead,
her eyes and mind are focused
on the beings evolving in our hands
as they inherit
names
personalities
and lore
from the four corners

of her ancestral imagination

but I'm struggling to stay in character,
struggling to stay rooted
in the here,
in the now

because every time one of our mini humans falls from our hands
and sails to the carpet below
I hear the crunching of bones
of skulls
of fibulas
of jaws
shattering beneath the brute force of
thin blue lines
and batons wielded by Klansmen with badges

even through the clouds of gas that send forest fires
screaming across our skin
I can see the fear
simmering in their eyes
The self-hatred and hunger
to dominate
to punish
to prove
to the flaming cross occupying space on the front lawns of their
fragile hearts and minds that
they are loyal
they are worthy
and maybe,
just maybe
master will them sleep in the house tonight

Tio!

her voice flash bangs through the room
sends thoughts scattering

What are you doing!?
It's time for a wardrobe change,
hurry up!

she scrambles to slip the dresses off our mini mannequins

but as she pulls them off

all I see are masks being pulled across
the faces of home-grown terrorists.

a DEI-approved spectrum of state-sanctioned bandits
armed with license to hunt and kill
the original caretakers of this land

ready to disappear mamis, tios, abuelos, hijos
into the ether,
rearrange their atoms into concentration camps
and one-way flights
    then report back,
    place their scalps on the scale,
    their tribute to the pale-skinned God of
    profit and plunder

Okay, hold on, hold on!
He has to put on this dress first.
Let me find it!

she rummages through her box looking for outfits,
pushing aside the parts of other dolls and toys

yet I can't push away the images
of mothers and fathers in Palestine
scavenging through remains of ancestral homes
gathering the body parts of their children in buckets
wondering if they'll be a ring, bracelet, or birthmark still left
to identify them by

entire family trees uprooted
and incinerated in makeshift furnaces
that were once schools
and hospitals,
transformed by heat-seeking drones
and seeds of steel that fall from the bellies of IOF warplanes
  bombs that still bear the lipstick and signatures
  of American politicians

I look back at her,
see the frustration building in her face
as she struggles to find the outfit
she has her heart set on

and wonder,

how do I communicate
that we are occupying space within belly of an empire
pressed between the pages of a centuries-old lie
passed down from slaveowners to CEO's?

that genocide and erasure
are embedded in the DNA strands of this country
tightly woven into a settler colonialist flag that has become
a symbol
a concept
that makes many of us,
or at least myself wonder,
is our planet really better off without
us?

Tio, I found it!!!

she holds a little dress up in her hand
her own emerald flag
that shimmers in the light,
and I see it,

I see revolution burning brightly in her eyes
infant stars shimmering
at the intersection
of past, present, and future.

I see visions for a new world
that rises from the ashes of capitalism and imperialism
a world,
without borders
without profit
without parents wondering
if they did the right thing
having children in the first place

I see revolution and resistance
guided by questions like:

How can I show up and take care of my community,
today?
How can I protect them from systems that can only survive because of our oppression
today?
How can I alleviate the suffering of my fellow human being–mi otro yo,
today?

questions we can answer in
our streets
our classrooms
our clinics
our libraries
our art spaces
our gardens
our kitchens
our living rooms
our relationships

questions we can answer
in every interaction we have with our planet
and our fellow human being,
because the two are one in the same

whatever pathway we feel compelled to take
to will this new world into existence
is sacred
and our own,
but we'll never get to our destination
by policing one another.
by turning our noses up at the mention
    of disruption
    of direct action
    of self-defense

remember,
peaceful resistance is only effective
when your oppressor has a conscious.

colonialism does not have a conscious
capitalism does not have a conscious
white supremacy does not have a conscious

also,
do these systems not inflict violence on the marginalized
every fucking moment of our existence?

is masked men kidnapping families and students in broad daylight
    not violence?
is eliminating access to healthcare, housing, food,
    not violence?
is erasing our histories and right to our identities
    not violence?
is sending billions of banknotes and bombs to ensure a genocidal crusade continues

not the literal definition of violence?

violence is never acceptable
when it's against
Property
Profit or
Whiteness.

instead
we're told to turn the cheek
with dignity and grace
turn it time and time again
till there's nothing left
but bruised flesh and bone
and even then,
if we still have something to say,
we must make sure to say it *respectfully*
and with a tone that would
never,
ever
make someone *uncomfortable.*

the state does not get to maintain a monopoly
on our methods of resistance

empire does not get to dictate
how people resist their very extinction

the oppressor does not–

Tio!

from thoughts of empire and revolution
i'm brought back to our living room
and to my niece explaining to me that somehow
our protagonists have been transformed
from dinner hosts into mermaids

I smile at the prospect of transformation
at all the potential ways I…
We,
might continue to show up
and transform this shared reality of ours
each and every day

because right now
all I want to do is just be here

with her,
and explain how yes,
this ken doll looks absolutely wonderful
in his emerald dress

By: Oscar Sandoval

Broken Silences

As internal silence becomes the rage that has engulfed me,
I cry tears of untold stories,
unable to express stifled emotions,
becoming the lost voice of previous generations.

I carry the weight of the world on my shoulders,
shifting its abundance to bear the pain—
and I never expected you to understand.

Broken pieces of shattered dreams
become the reality of my existence,
validating my presence as just another burden.

My heart has become incarcerated,
unable to love another,
because I'm still trying to figure out what love is.

On the brink of another night of confusion,
searching, and solitude,
I bear witness to the angst of not being accepted.

My selflessness is mistaken for selfishness,
because my good has been evil spoken of.

And, in a search for redemption,
I prove myself a thousand times
only to be called a contradiction.

Who am I?
A question that haunts me but renders no answers.

However, my search continues—
tired of shedding tears of oppression,
because I matter.

Years of misunderstanding
become the foundation for conflict,
as ignorance becomes the new source of evil.

Perhaps if you walked a mile or two in my shoes,
you'd understand that my story is composed of more
than just a fairy tale and a happy ending.

As the rising action leads to the climax,
there are many tears cried and much blood lost,
but conclusion never really resolves anything.

So, is this all in vain?
Is this all in vain?
Is this all in vain?
Because I've lived in silence for too long,
and I must have a voice.

By: Maestro DeSean

Diferencias

From this side of the border,
I see the Mexican flag,
moving to the sound waves of corridos and banda.
People cross barbed wire-laced rivers and are labeled illegal and undocumented.
When they came from Europe, they were labeled conquistadors, explorers, and holy men.
My hands are clasped in forced prayer to a god who leaves my fate up to cotton fields that hide the bodies of fellow sisters.
Sometimes I long to fly,
Soar like a golden eagle with an asp in its mouth and go beyond patrolled chain-linked fences.
To pluck me out of these lands where children plan
the best places to hide when a shooter decides today's the day.
To avoid looking up into the infinite darkness of a barrel
that swallows them into the black holes of politics.
Outside police argue about what time's the time to do something.
I raise my gaze towards moons that block the sun.
From out the past, so does my ancestor.
The riverbeds and valleys of our palms touch.
Spaces between our arms are shaped like the pyramids that mirror the stars.
My face holds the tell-tale signs of successful invasions.
But my heart holds the persistence of wilder, stronger blood.
There's a longing in my heart to be there.
If I leave, I can't take this life with me.
Wings only carry you so far into Mictlan.

By: Christiane Williams-Vigil

Generations

Before men and women were going on strike standing on the front-lines with Cesar Chavez screaming "Si se puede!" Yes We Can,

My great-grandfather was starting his own revolution
teaching himself to read and write English
by rummaging through school-yard trash cans for used spelling books and old newspapers

My grandfather came
over
from Míchoacan, México
to pick cotton in California
he even helped build the Kansas City Railroad
but ended up
being too Mexican
to ride the trains that flew across the tracks
of his hard labor

And who would have thought,
my father
little brown hands picking grapes in the Fresno heat would be the first in our family
to graduate high school and
end up building satellites for NASA

Yet,
you
El Presidente can sit the owner of lives,
tell me
that we are replaceable

That there is a cake that your mother is baking
that needs the perfect sized strawberries

that we don't deserve more than fifteen-minute-break-a-day
because money doesn't grow on trees
moneydoesn'tgrowontrees

money,
doesn't grow
on trees

Well
neither does blood
neither do brown hands

neither does courage
neither does strength
neither do weaknesses

You ask me
the third generation
of the Brown-blood-gone-light
if I am ashamed of this heritage,

I can tell you, señor
I don't hear shame calling me in my sleep
I don't hear shame in 3am phone calls to
My father,
"Papi,
I'm working three jobs and
I just can't take it anymore
Papi,
I get down on my knees everyday
not to pray to God
But to clean up after people's shit
And I just can't take it anymore
Papi,
I can't make my rent again next month
And I am livin' just enough for the city
And I just can't take it anymore"

I don't hear shame
When my father tells me,
Mija,
Haven't you learned by now
their are fields of solderos,
Soldiers swimming through your veins
Mija,
Don't you know
that there are reasons why the Universe
only gives you as much as you can carry
Mija,
There are fields of things
that your heart
already knows

And this I know:
I have crawled across the backs of men and women
just so I could climb back into the womb
of a mother-country
so I could be re-born and say to you:

You Do Not Plant These Seeds
You Do Not Own These Roots
Your Government Does Not Birth This Fruit

So don't tell me
how I don't understand the taste of the sweetest red grapes on a sunny August morning
because trust me,

they are filled
with the blood and sweat
of three generations of Aztec warriors
And I've come to know
what the truth
tastes like.

By: Meliza Bañales

On the thought of being taken away

In the absence of nothing we have encapsulated everything
the empty silence fills the room like the ocean on a Rubik's cube –
the unintentional movements always lead to the final version
of the clouds where I always think of the end --
of the moment I am living –
no one told me there is never a stop
only a consecutive pause

By: Maria Duarte

Swimming

the water is not clear
but the water is never clear
the fish swim in it anyways,
do the fish go blind from the sand?
No, the sand never stays in the surface,
do we swim through darkness
or do we sink hopeless like sand?

By: Maria Duarte

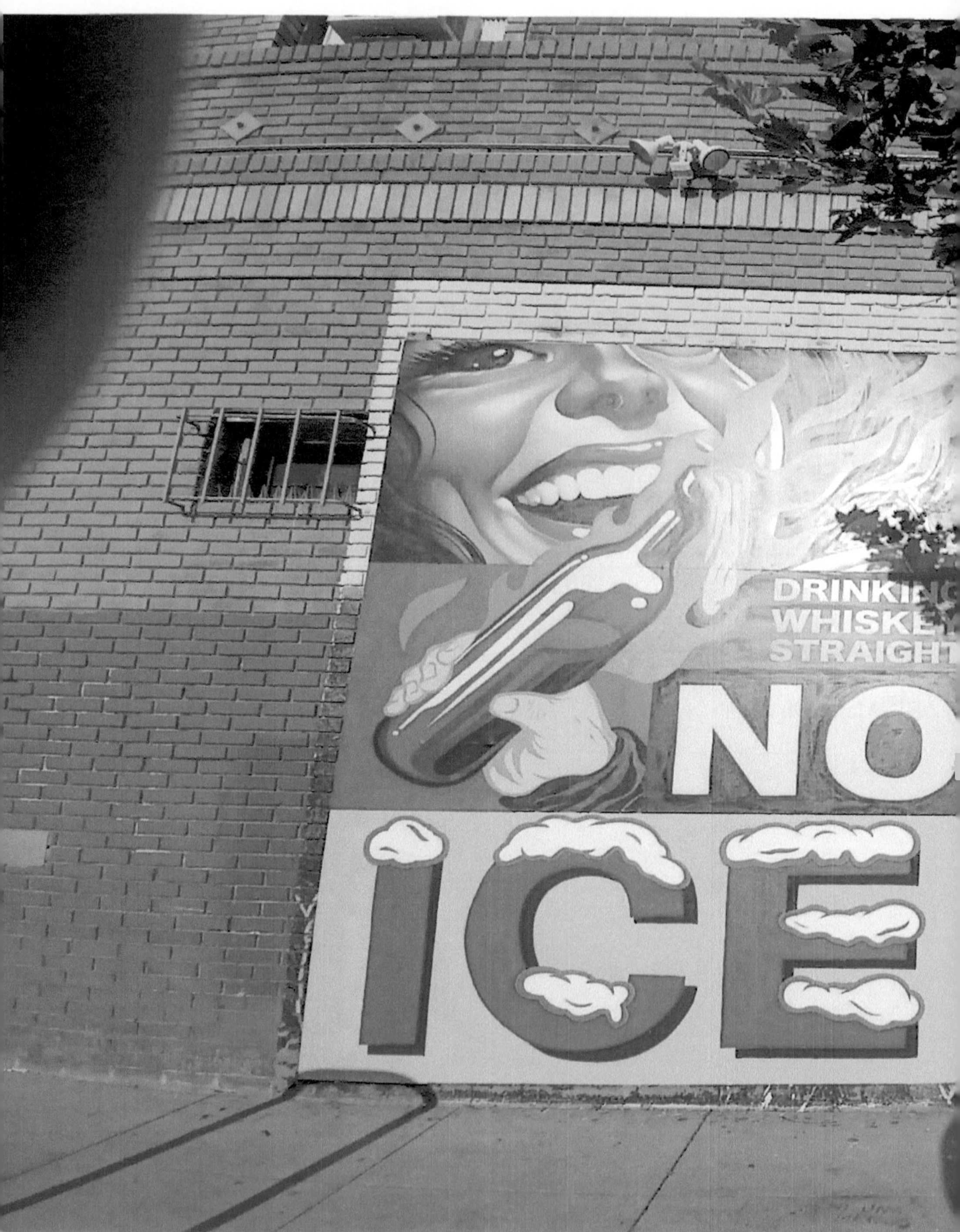

By: Gia Civerolo

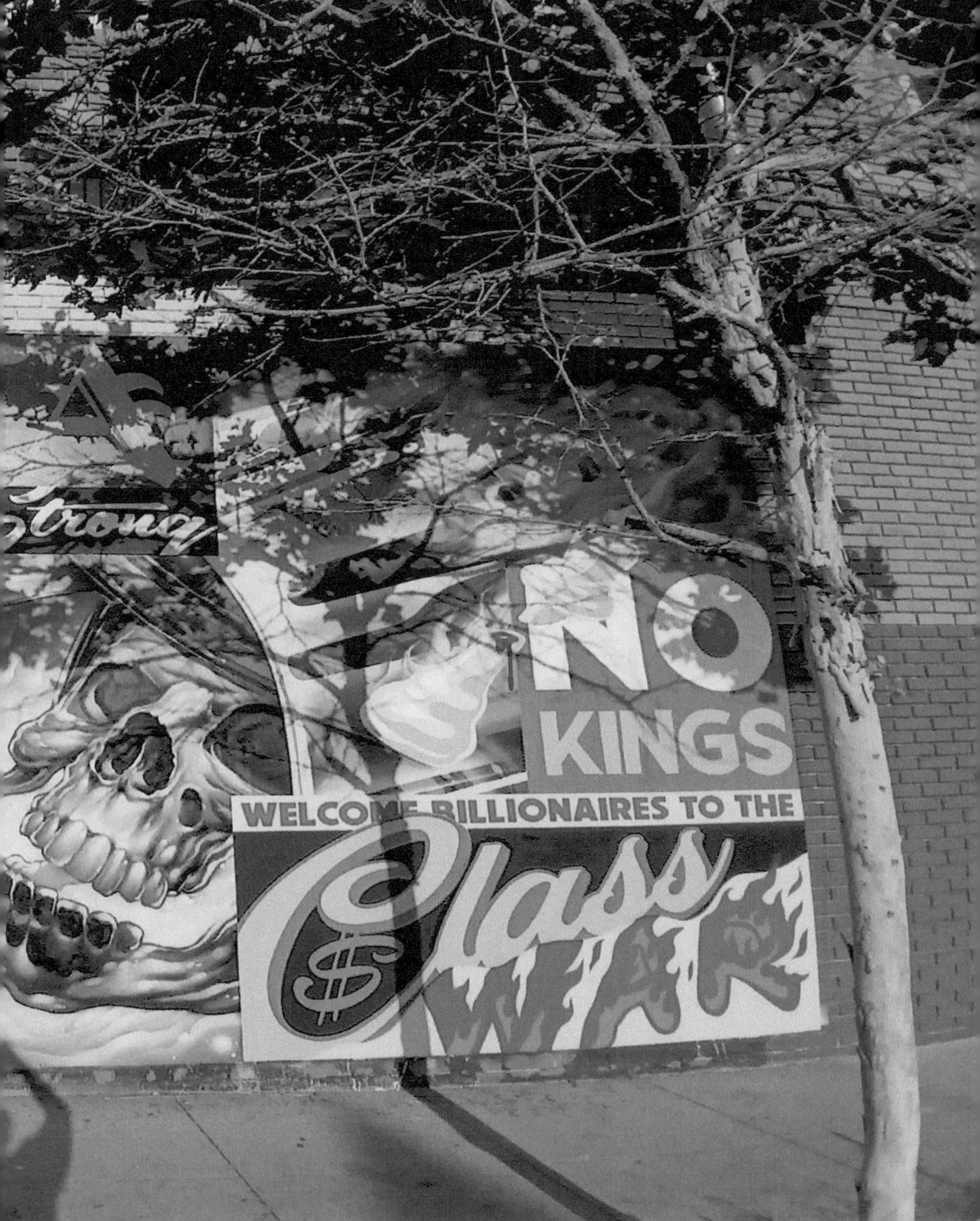
Strong
NO
KINGS
WELCOME BILLIONAIRES TO THE
Class
WAR

My dearest America

What happened to you?

You were the land of the free
You were hope for immigrants
Given to us by Lady Liberty

When did money become so important?

When did big companies convince you,
That humans did not matter.

Citizens are dying

And America cares about making money

Money for big companies
Money for the wealthy
Money for billionaires to thrive

But we, the forgotten people

Whose ancestors traveled
difficult journeys

To live here
To breathe here
To work here
To survive here

Tell me, America,
When did your heart harden?

When did your kindness,
your love,
your hope
turn into *greed*

When Covid hit,
It was your people of color
Your poor
Your people without healthcare
dying

And still your 1%
Your billionaires
Thrived and profited

But us, the ones of color,
the poor
lost their jobs
And watched our loved ones die
around us

Where were you, America?
When tragedy was striking people dead

And the wealthy,
the big companies,
the billionaires
Stood there and did nothing

It was Poe's *Masque of the Red Death*,

Where Prince Prospero had an extravagant party
While everyone on the outside was bleeding to death

Us, your people of color bled to death

And the blood spilled on our infants
The cycle continued

With no hope for change

I am American, but ½ a citizen
Like my brothers and sisters of color

Who have been marginalized
Who have suffered,
Who have been downtrodden

Greed is more important

Than me living
Than my children thriving
Than my human seed surviving
Greed has stolen you America

Transformed you into the land of the struggle

And today you have Gestapo
ICE running around
Stealing lives
Lives of innocent people
Who work hard and just want
A chance

A chance to a life they are beholden to
Because their land was stolen

Lawless men with masks
Committing crimes against humanity

In this great country

Grandmas and grandpas taken
Children taken
Men and women taken
Innocent lives taken

And for what to appease
Are so called President
Who only cares about the wealthy
And no one else matters

I met a brave soul the other day
A Snow Cone/Corn/Chip seller
Brave enough to go to a basketball court
Surrounded by police
The league is sponsored by Montebello Pd
And yet, there he stood

Trying to feed his family
Trying to live his life
In the midst of all the Ice Raids
There he stood

Defying it all

A man of character and integrity
Risking it all because his family needs to eat

America, you have lost yourself

As we grieve the injustices
With so much disillusionment
So much pain

Together as humans
We will stand together
And rise

And scream

No more!

By: Erica Castro

TENDER AND WILD,

Previously published in A Speaker is a Wilderness: Poems on the Sacred Path from Broken to Whole by Anna Goodman Herrick

like my mother:
Earth. Within me, the storm,
the wreckage,
whole communities sprout up
to find each other, make ceremony
for our dead, nurse the gasping

back to life. New houses are built
in me. Protests.
Whole uprisings. I am made
of multitudes
that cannot be contained.

By: Anna Goodman Herrick

DIASPORA PRAYER OF THE REFUGEE'S GRANDCHILD

Previously published in A Speaker is a Wilderness: Poems on the Sacred Path from Broken to Whole by Anna Goodman Herrick

"Diaspora Prayer Of The Refugee's Grandchild" first appeared in Life as Ceremony, Curator Alice Baca.

I know how to wrap my hair in a scarf, black and abloom
with fuchsias and call myself my own grandmother.

I know there are a thousand names for G-d
bound around tongues

and a thousand ways to say my name
in all the languages I have longed for, from the
places I have tried to call home.

I know I am a guest unsought in a stolen
guest house and the refugee

who lives on in my blood took shelter
built from an occupier's dream of home. I know
this is not a prayer to be spoken lightly.

I know my frame remains a visitor, provisional
and the God alive in my body took shelter
built from an ad exec's imagination of a woman

and this Limitless is demolishing
and rebuilding her. I know when the Sacred
asks her to leave, she will have to listen. I know
when the Sacred asks her to leave she will have to listen.

I know I am already an ancestor and it's time
to act accordingly. Somewhere, the future
is remembering me.

By: Anna Goodman Herrick

[if your heart is broken let it keep breaking]

Previously published in A Speaker is a Wilderness: Poems on the Sacred Path from Broken to Whole by Anna Goodman Herrick

if your heart is broken let it keep breaking let it shatter
into a million pieces let it shard let it cut
you wide open you will never be the same
and sometimes this can be a good thing your tears
yes will salt your wounds for a while we have all
been torn open by each other let yourself come be the wound
opening you will embrace the world this way

By: Anna Goodman Herrick

THE WHOLE STORY

Previously published in A Speaker is a Wilderness: Poems on the Sacred Path from Broken to Whole by Anna Goodman Herrick

In her kitchen wallpapered in violets,
my grandmother warns me to love
everyone, to never hate

anyone's skin, tradition or country –
not after the decimation that found her family.

To know that other marks the beginning of death,
to know this separation transforms us humans into
the murderers and the murdered in minutes.

This is the way I learn to love,
begin to carry an open heart
caged in bones soaked in terror.

I will spend years renaming the plot —
love because love is who you are.
That's it. That's the whole story.

By: Anna Goodman Herrick

BLESSING FOR DIASPORA AS A SPIRITUAL PRACTICE

Previously published in A Speaker is a Wilderness: Poems on the Sacred Path from Broken to Whole by Anna Goodman Herrick

"Blessing For Diaspora As A Spiritual Practice" first appeared in Ritualwell.

To be alive
is to attend a prayer service.
To do the work of the heart
in the temple of the world,
to build
the tender center of that temple
inside yourself,
is a blessing:
to seek for that center again and again
in everyone, each body a tent for conducting
its own ceremony into ascension,
to build the altar within you
and decide what you will sacrifice
and who you will not,
to hold all the brokenness
for the sake of any chance of repair,
to welcome everyone exiled,
everything broken
from its origins,
all holiness ripped
from its dwelling places,
and chant together,
here, here, here.

By: Anna Goodman Herrick

Big bad Government

Big bad government may I have your undivided attention?
There's just a couple things that I would like to mention.
I understand that I'm just a mere spec on the face of this earth.
But I can bear witness to the nation's abuse since birth.
Could you ever stand to get off your podium on Capitol hill?
Step down and truly observe for my people what's always been real?
In my short-lived journey of life I've seen your kind come through here before,
making promises of a better living and fucking the people up more.
Suppressing the poor.
I could have sworn that the government was down for the people.
So why this constant oppression of my people?
The Constitution states that all men are created equal.
But the history bears truth to a reality that's lethal.
I'm sick of the shit about being politically correct,
when the people keep getting screwed and the government's erect.
I just feel the need as a young seed of this nation,
to interject and expose the threats of not being
young, rich, prissed and Caucasian.
And no I don't have a racist a bias or a bitter mentality.
I just chose to expose myself to the bitter realities.
Like how the quality for lower class is constantly overlooked.
How my public school classes remain constantly overbooked.
With overused books and underpaid teachers.
A generation that took to the streets filled with false prophets and preachers.
These Divine systems of government that are supposed to serve
and protect chooses to disrespect and neglect.
Hand the silver platter to those with already a couple to store upon display.
It's like we're getting hung like in the olden days.
The ways of the government are trashed away, we're trashed and slain.
Revealing them as the predator and the people to prey.
Speech after speech promising new days, and new ways.
Then we see little to no progression that's our government's oppression.
They say that I'm lessened due to the color of my skin, and uncommitted sins.
Then again, I fully intend to be neglected and rejected by a system of government
only claiming to serve and protect.
That's why we keep getting screwed and the government's erect.
Big bad government can hear a plea not just coming from a woman,
once a little girl, born a minority. Who would flip through her textbooks with
numerous pages missing and then try to pass the chapter test by just guessing.
Big bag government cuz you stand and get off your podium on Capitol hill.
Step down and truly observe for my people it's always been real?

By: Jamie Maxwell

The Stripper vs. the president

The stripper asked for my consent
But not the president

I said yes to the stripper
Never to this president

My flexibility on full display
Cheerleader splits

Little men gaze, lording power
Jealous of creation

I said yes to the stripper
Respectful to the ownership

My body, my choice
She would never just grab

My pussy without asking
No one grabs my pussy without asking

I am God damn glad to live
In a state that guards my choice

While the nation is ruled by oppression
My body and health are borders I guard

The stripper asked for my consent
While also getting her PHD

My body My choice
My body My choice

Margaret Atwood never
Dreamed the "Handmaid's Tale"

Would become so true dystopian
world for our daughters to navigate

The stripper asked for my consent
She knows true pleasure comes from a yes

Rape is torture not your fantasy
Dumb ass president

The stripper asked me for my consent
No means no Mr. President

By: Gia Civerolo

The Commander of Empire

There's a person I know who has been separated
from their family because of the ice raids.
I know they will return to their family
because of the next commander of empire.

A person I know has a nephew whose father returned to him
because of the previous commander of empire.

This person with the nephew.
His father was sent out of this farce
because of the commander of empire when the pandemic first hit.

When the next one became commander of empire,
bringing aspects of Adventure Time to real life,
the father embarked on a quest to return to the farce to see his son again.

All this to say, this person, who asked the moon to enter the windows of their soul will soon go on a path to return to the farce

to return with their family once more.

By: Jesse Tovar

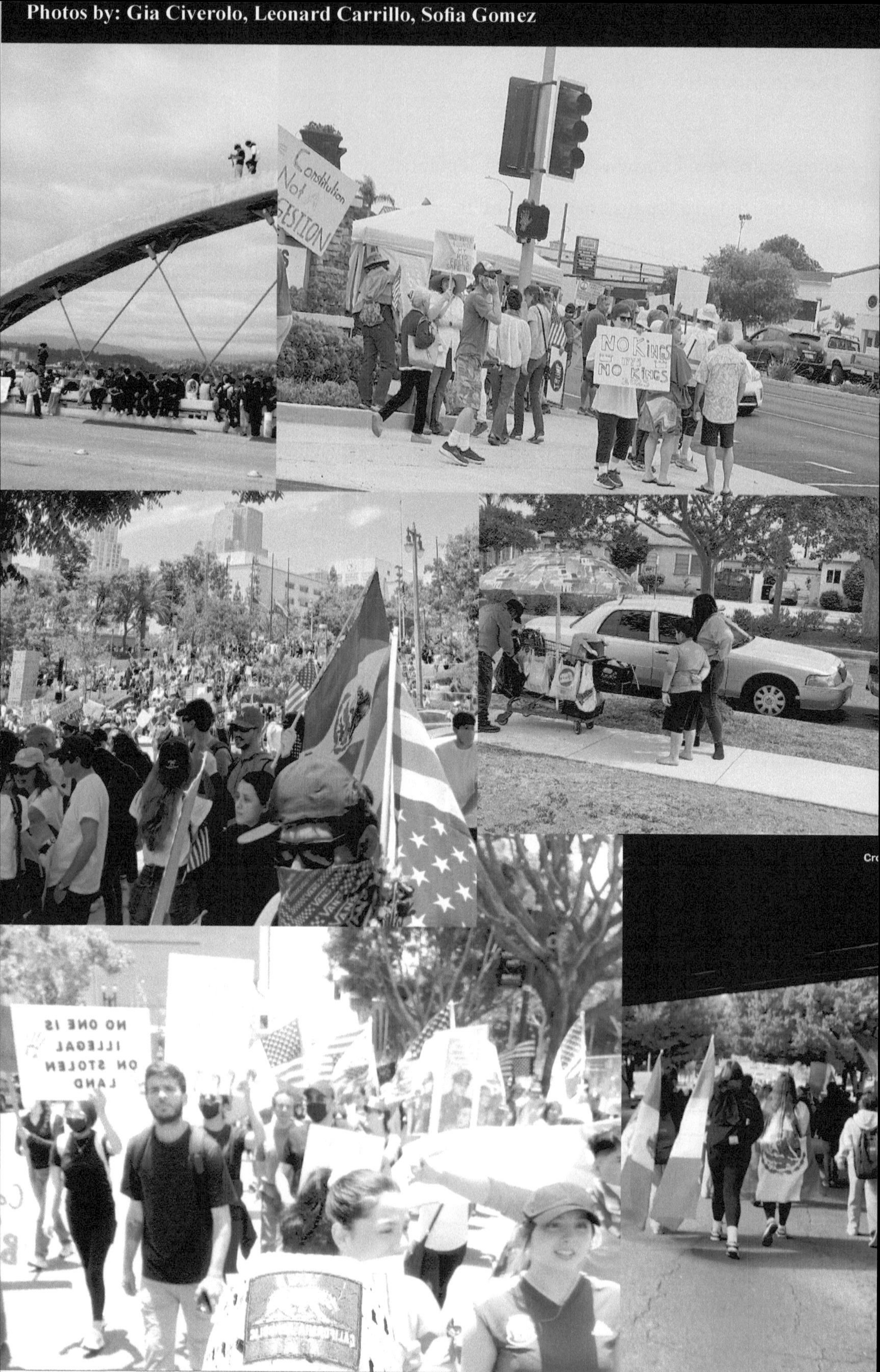

Photos by: Gia Civerolo, Leonard Carrillo, Sofia Gomez

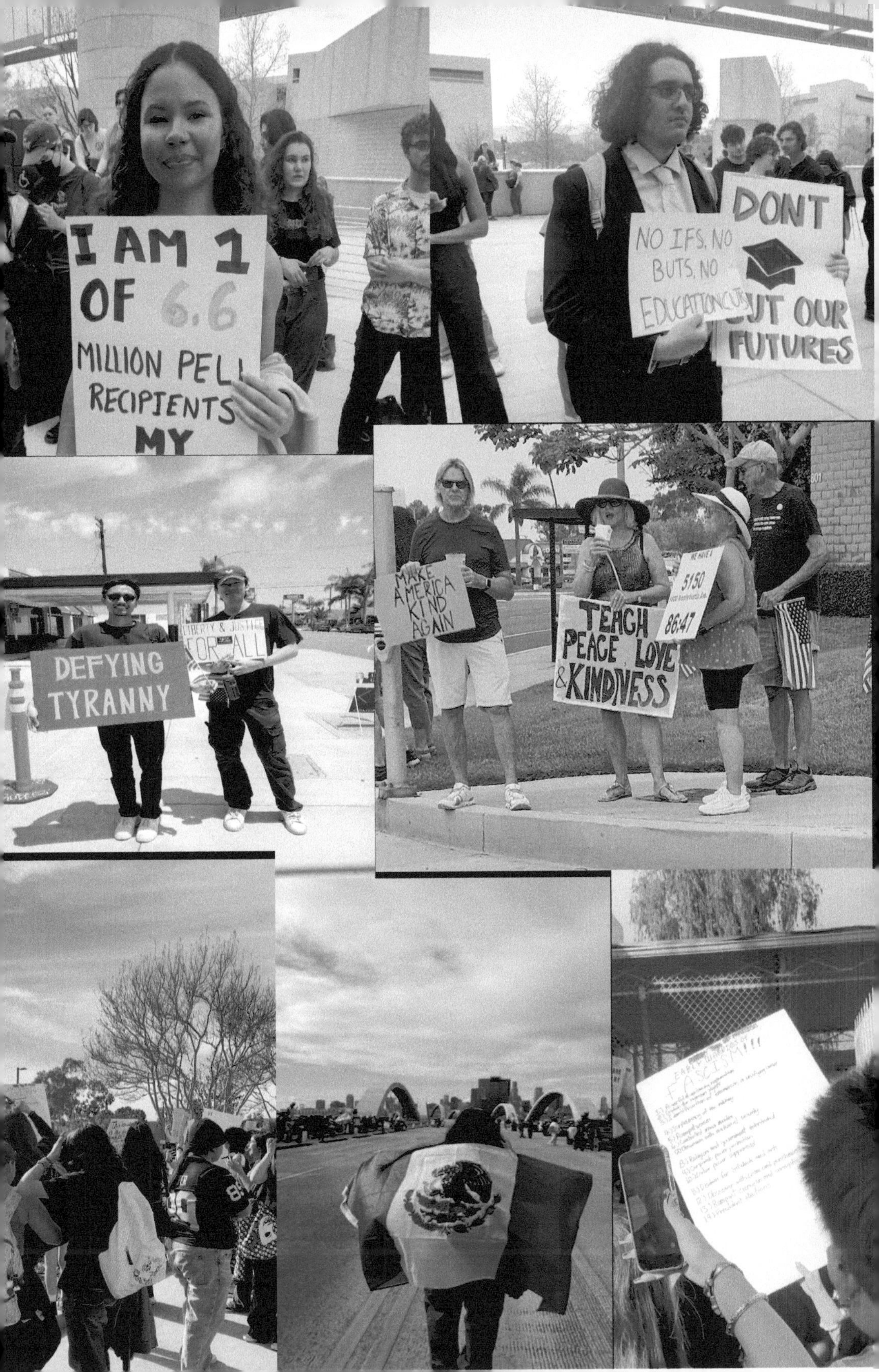
I AM 1 OF 6.6 MILLION PELL RECIPIENTS MY
NO IFS, NO BUTS, NO EDUCATION CUTS
DONT
UT OUR FUTURES
DEFYING TYRANNY
LIBERTY & JUSTICE FOR ALL
MAKE AMERICA KIND AGAIN
TEACH PEACE, LOVE & KINDNESS
5150
86:47
FASCISM

“Palabra”

Keep trucha,it’s operation Wetback II
see the settler back at it
again to fuck you
or your tio o tia,
si chinga la migra

Olmecas crushin Tesla
in Oaxaca La Venta
y si, fuera los gringos de
Tenochtitlan
condesa, la roma,

where they don’t belong
it’s a rising Godzilla
Bell, Pico Rivera
in defense of la tierra,

familia Tolteca

ya basta, la mierda
just struck the fan
shady masked mother fuckers
in the black ice van
dem devils crazy,
kidnapping tamale ladies,
they’ll get us into raging
when we see the agents staging
in the dark,
at McArthur Park,
in Paramount they got checked
cuz Cuitlahuac’s not dead
Maya tata’s got friends
from LA to the Peten
Belen y Mario
tambien la Rosario!

By: Tezozomoc

“Dear Frontera”

Dear Frontera,
You should’ve never covered your toes with barbed wire
Your eyes with chain-link fence
Your ankles with detention centers
They used you to cut themselves from Latin America
You are an open wound
A self-mutilation
They try to use ICE to soothe the pain.

Dear Frontera,
You are a cinch ever tightening
A rack ever pulling
A metal wall extending into the ocean off the coast of Baja
A string of buoys covered with blades for the drowning in Tejas.

Dear Frontera,
You are the bride
Of a nation of sadists.

By: David Romero

“Querida frontera”

Querida frontera,
Nunca deberías haberte cubierto los dedos de los pies con alambre de púas.
Tus ojos con una cerca de tela metálica
Tus tobillos con los centros de detención
Te utilizaron para aislarse de América Latina
eres una herida abierta
Una automutilación
Usar ICE/hielo para calmar el dolor

Querida frontera,
Eres muy fácil de apretar
Un estante siempre tirando
Un muro de metal que se extiende hacia el océano frente a la costa de Baja California
Una hilera de boyas cubiertas con palas para los ahogados en Tejas

Querida frontera,
tu eres la novia
De un país de sádicos.

Por: David Romero

The Battle of Los Angeles

The spirits of the Brown Berets have blessed the streets of OUR LADY of the angels…

We are gathered here to protect our raza.
We were gathered here to ask for payment for our blood & sweat but they wanted our tears so they attacked tired brown eyes with chemical agents.
Used rubber bullets made from foreign labor.
Rubbers impregnating our skin; domestic violence bruises delivered by those who are supposed to protect and serve.

The children of the SUN are done living under a racist shadow of red, white and blue.
We were told to stop speaking our native language.
We were told our skin was too dark to qualify for human decency.

Our Fathers, Our Mothers, My Abuelita, Mi Abuelito have all died several deaths under this American sun.
We were dragged from our neighborhoods in the 30's, 40's, 60's and then gang profiled in the 90's.

Our veins make up the Aztec golden thread woven into the LA scene. So how can our fabric be illegal?

We work at your sweat shops. We sew your flag.
Without us this city unravels. Without us our brown seeds will never become chicano palm trees.
LA smog should never be made up of tear gas bombs.
THIS is a call for action for the city of Los Angeles ;that we the Mexicans REFUSE to be erased from our land again.

IF we pick the fruit.
IF we watch your children.
IF we we fix your cars.
Don't tell me this land isn't ours.
The Battle of Los Angeles has always been won when RAGE meets hard working brown hearts.
Our people. Mi Familia. Stands Together.
No Contaban con mi AUDACITY.
Pero Aqui Estamos Bilingue y con corazon de un pueblo unido.

The spirits of the Brown Berets that came before us will forever protect esta lucha de piel Morena.

We carry the fire in our breath and the ancestors voices on microphones still waiting for us to revolt again.
Chicana por dentro. Chicano por fuera. Mexican American skin holds LA's history hasta el FIN.

By Sandy Shakes

A Battle's Cry

It was never ours
to rest—
that is our worth
the inability to
be we are magic

if we do it right,
we can make ourselves

invisible

oh I never would have guessed
I didn't mean you you don't look
you don't act you don't seem

until
you do.

We the quiet people
siesta in the shade. Right?

In the papers they once called us
the sleeping giant
in the papers our children are described
by color and tragedies
white children described by achievement or
lone wolf sharpshooter

but not us

we are the unrested

and when we rise in a tri-color flag
commemorating that ride
from the mythical north
to the mythical south
snake in talon and beak

we are told to go back
and ignore the broken treaty
caked in blood and dust

and when they say
we were made for labor
we toil in justice & raised fists
we were born for unrest
we were born for now

from the whitest of us hiding
to the darkest unable to
we raise our fist

& we shall not be moved.

By: Margaret Elysia Garcia

Detention Centers

My name is Nina, short for Evangelina
I am ocho años
I crossed the border with a coyote
Before we got captured
I am currently in Clint, Texas
A Detention facility
I am in charge of a two year old little girl
It is my job to protect her because
A man comes and takes some of the other girls
And they do not come back the same
I am eight, but I understand. The older girls
Say it is abuse
I am not sure what, exactly, I just get a sick feeling
In my stomach.
I came to be with my mom
It has been cuatro años
Since she crossed, so we can have a better life
But we got caught
We are riddled with piojos
The policemen got mad because we lost the piojo comb
I know piojos
We are not supposed to share the comb
But they only gave us one,
And we all have piojos
They do not care they feed us maruchan sopa
Avena en el microondas
Comida hecha con agua
A little girl died we do not know how
Something tells me she was killed
There are people who are willing to pick us up
I have a tía, a tío, mi mamá
But this government will not permit it
They think we are better off detained
But they keep us here being abused and touched
By these cochino men
The babies are taken care of by the teenagers
They do not have enough pampers
They do not let us take a shower
This is a better life?
I would have rather stayed with abuelita
I just missed mamá so much
Now I am stuck here hungry, dirty, and with piojos
This is what this country does to all the little immigrant girls
We are dangerous…I do not know how
They keep us in these cold cells
We sleep on the floor

There are sick children
They give them Tylenol
Two times a day
But the kids are still sick
I am eight, but I know this is wrong

Children suffering because this great
Country see immigrant children as a threat
No parents, no rights,
Just trapped behind these dreaded walls

By: Erica Castro

Roots in the Dirt

This August marks 504 years of European invasion and destruction of Our Ancestros
The ashes of destruction they brought forth were intended to annihilate
Surely, they thought it was the end of us
But they didn't know we were seeds
Seeds that continued to plant more seeds within Madre Tierra
For centuries before and after the invasion
Under the dirt,
We sprouted, grew, and waited.

The savage Europeans tried to sever and cut us from our culture, uproot us completely
They burned our books – note why a group would do something such as destroy literature –
They created a caste system and put our skin color below them
They created ideology that shackled Our Indigenous Minds
Justifying abuse, murder, genocide in a different time and place,
After 504 years of hatred, jealousy, and despair
They are still trying to rid us through means of tactics
Through means of incarceration, dogmatic religion, Eurocentric favoritism
And brainwashing to hate Ourselves – and it's worked for many, many years.

But Our Ancestros danced, sang, and told stories
Just as we all dance, sing, and tell stories within Our Comunidad
Look around you right now and feel the energy we are producing, even if you are alone,
We are medicine that heals,
All of this is to help us realize that Our Culture was never completely destroyed
No European steel could ever completely sever Our Indigenous Roots
That are so wholesome and abundant from Our Tierra.

Our People are remembering, and I hope this prayer helps you to remember
As I am still remembering
A cultural amnesia we are slowly awakening from years of suppressed oppression
By the same genocidal acts that were committed half a century ago.
We all must remember who we are and where we come from and why we should represent, us,
Not just from Mexico,
Nuestros hermanos y hermanas de El Salvador, Guatamala, Honduras, Nicaragua,
Toda la Tierra del Sur y toda la Isla de la Tortuga,

Todos los que son de aqui y todos los inmigrantes, no es importante.
They cannot stand the fact that we still exist
I proudly stay visible with My Roots shown,
I hope you will proudly stay visible with Y(Our) Roots shown,
Especially for those that remain invisible today.

By: Jake Teran

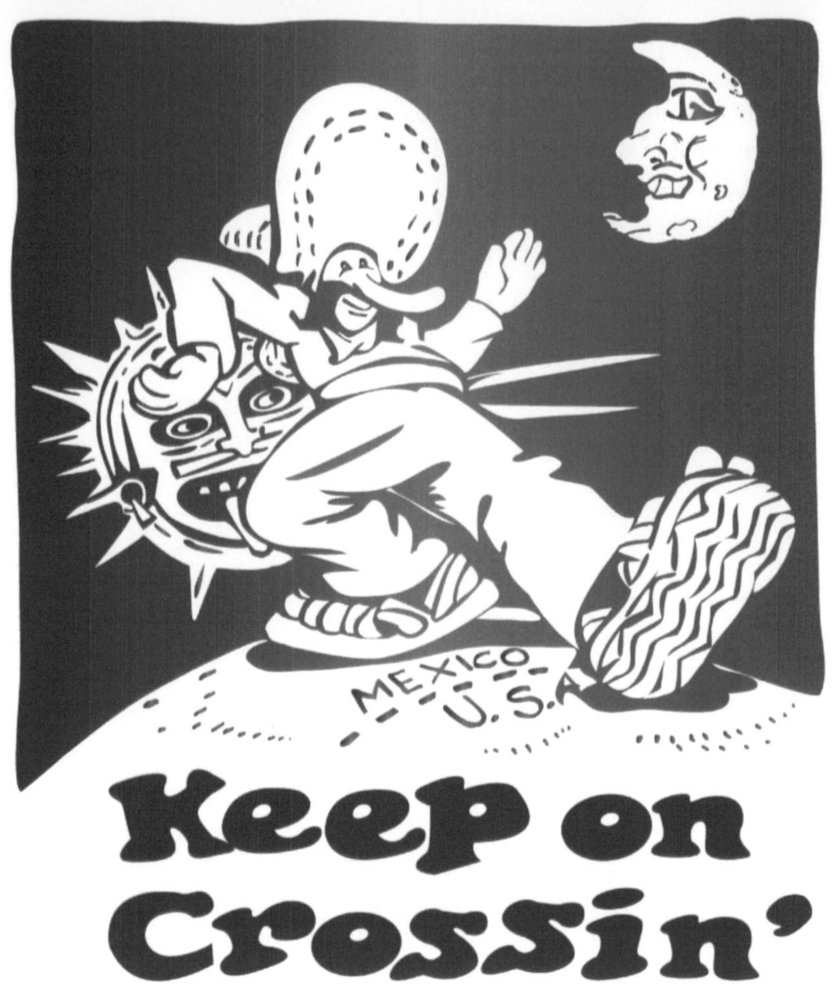

Keep on Crossin' Manifesto

When in the course of human events it becomes necessary to cross borders of political, social, linguistic, cultural, economic and technological construction...we will cross. For long before there were borders, there were crossers. We are the proud sons and daughters of these crossers, and we hold that crossing is a basic human right. Furthermore, we hold this right to be in-illegal alienable.

Artificial borders of body and mind and spirit must be crossed off the list. For every star-crossed, cross-bearing, cross-platform, cross-dressing, cross-country, cross-walker at the crossroads of culture, the time has come to cross.

We are living in a time when a truckload of toxic waste has more rights to cross than a human being. Wherever and whenever this is the case, we will cross.

Our crossing will be a sign to other crossers that the time has come to cross. We will cross at intersections. Anywhere we cross will become an intersection by the act of our crossing. We will look both ways before crossing, and then, with the positive momentum of humanity, we will cross.

We will cross into other manifestos. These include but are not limited to the Prague Manifesto for Esperanto, the Russell-Einstein Manifesto against nuclear war, the Roxy Music song "Manifesto," the Universal Declaration of Human Rights, the Plan of Delano, the Plan Espiritual de Aztlan and any other plans, declarations or manifestos that encourage, promote and reward crossing.

When the border expands, we contract. And when the border contracts, we expand. And when it is time to cross, we will cross all by ourselves.

Wherever there are tired, huddled masses yearning to breathe free, we will cross.

Wherever there's a cop beatin' up a guy, we will cross.

As Martin Luther King wrote from the injustice stained confines of a Birmingham jail: "We are caught in an inescapable network of mutuality, tied in a single garment of destiny."

By wearing this patch, we declare that our garment be counted as a piece from Dr. King's "single garment of destiny."

And to ensure that the sun and moon continue to shine on the smiling faces of the free, we will keep on crossing.

By: Victor Payan © 2003

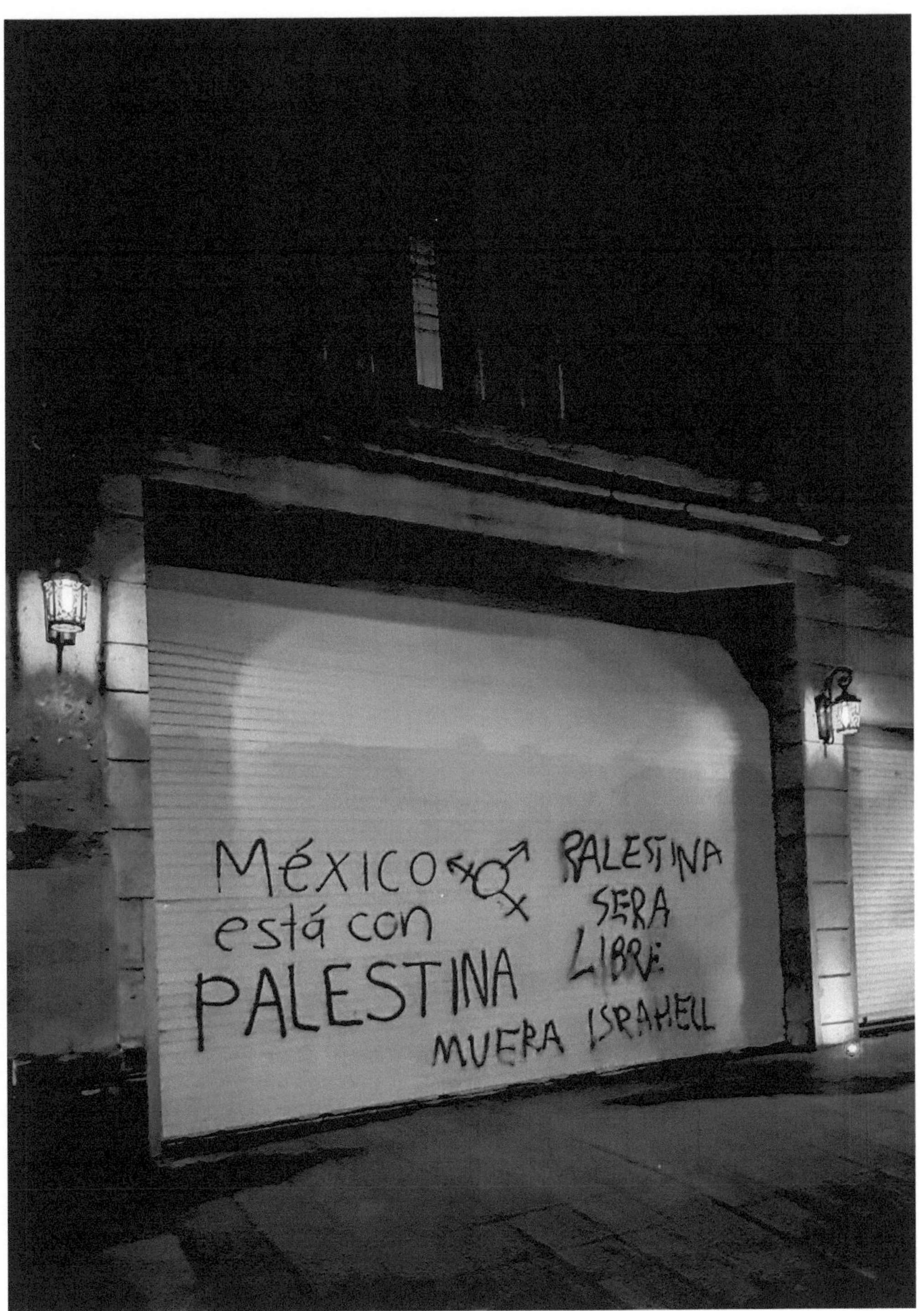

By: Arturo Meza

STOP THE GENOCIDE IN PALESTINE NOW! (AUGUST 11, 2025)

I am Palestinian.

I wasn't born in Palestine. I don't have direct lineage to the people who've lived there for thousands of years. I'm Palestinian because I'm human. Their ancestors are my ancestors as "mine" are theirs. During the Holocaust, I was Jewish. I wasn't born during the Nazi genocide of Jews (I was born some ten years after the end of the Third Reich). But when they were being exterminated it impacted me tremendously.

I'm human. We have the same ancestors in the great human lineage of all ancestors.

When Africans were stolen from their homes as part of the Transatlantic slave trade, I never saw the inside of a slave ship or lived on the terrible plantations where they lost everything to help build this so-called country called "America." But I was one of them.

I was Irish during the English colonialization and the famine. I was Lakota, Haudenosaunee (Mohawk), Laguna, Diné, and Chumash when their lands and livelihoods were taken away by European powers.

They are all my people.

How can I say this? Borders, nations, languages, belief systems—they came later. They were created under distinct historical circumstances, but what's common about us is greater than what distinguishes us. Everyone has their stories, values, histories, expressions. Unique and valid. They are all human. Like me.

If you must know my genealogy, from at least 1,000 years, I'm Indigenous with roots in original Mexican peoples such as the Rarámuri, Chichimecas, and Nahuas (different peoples, different idioms, different myths). But we are all one.

I also have Iberian, other European, and African DNA. It's all good and important to know. But I wasn't born "fractured" or "mixed," with "this blood and that blood." My blood is human. I'm not "mestizo" (part of the Spanish casta system). I was whole and complete the day I was born.

While some in the U.S. have called me "foreigner," "alien," and "stranger" (and worse things than that); while a teacher slapped my face at six years old for speaking Spanish (another colonial language like English) in a Watts public school; while police harassed me in my barrio neighborhood in the San Gabriel Valley of Los Angeles County in the 1960s and early 1970s when Mexican migrant barrios were as poor as the Deep South, Appalachia, or any Indigenous Reservation (most of area is now "gentrified")—and I lost four friends to police violence—my roots run deep.

I belong here and everywhere.

Am I bitter? No. I'm beyond "victimhood." I embody a spirit of resistance, a revolutionary, who will fight for the liberation of the planet and its people—to remove all chains of social class, race, ethnicity, gender, sex, and whatever other oppressions have held us down for centuries.

I'm human above all else. I'm an Earth being. I'm for the whole integrated earth and sky systems. People-made systems are only any good if they align with these other natural and truly long-lasting systems. When they don't, I will fight back—think, study, write, and organize.

I have agency. I'm human.

Israel and the United States are made up entities, no matter what Zionists or Christian Nationalists/MAGA may claim. Neither "God" or "manifest destiny" created them. They were founded on genocide. Israel against Palestine. United States against the original peoples of the land. Although I'm a U.S. citizen, I also have my own mind and heart: I'm critical of those entanglements that draw from and celebrate this history, this genocide.

Any genocide. All genocide.

Countries come and go. Humans continue. Parties and allegiances serve minimal and narrow things. Any religion does the same—except for the expansive and embracing believers, it's their "god," "their" rituals, "their" laws. Good for them, but not for everyone.

So as a human, beyond borders, country, or party, I say along with most of the world: We must stop the Genocide in Palestine. In any part of this planet. We are human first. Remember that. Not “America” first. Or this or that religion “first.” Or this piece of real estate “first.” We are one as human beings. Like the Yucatan Mayans say: “In Lak’ech, Ala K’in”—You are the other me; I’m the other you.

I’m Palestinian. Stop the Genocide now!

By: Luis J. Rodriguez

Oh Palestine

Sweet Peas
Their scent is what I
want to bring to my sister.
The wooden frame to support
the fragrant vine,
I dream it to be a
bridge so that I may visit her
with news of our mother.

And I bring her
a plump bouquet of sweet
lavender, pink, and blue.
How can I give them to my beloved sister?

I will build a perfumed bridge with a
lattice wall of Sweet Pea vines.
The vine's tendril points remind me
of the barbed wire, fortressed across

my Palestine,
my little town
across my back yard,
across my heart.

"Oh Palestine." Altadena Poetry Review: Anthology, 2024.

By: Vibiana Aparicio-Chamberlin

Mother and Child of Gaza

I wish for you a peach
with fine fuzz to stroke your cheeks
and juice to quench your thirst
and its fragrance on your tongue

I go now. My heart valves tire of pumping
blood of worthless blue. I feel spent, but my love
is strong endless. I desire for you a painless passage.
With my every last drop of blood, I wish you smiles
and the sight of white butterflies before
the gossamer veil covers your darling eyes
I will sing 'Awaken my child, awaken.'

no more sounds of rocket bombs
only songs of love and
only a baby lullaby
in the other world

if you go after me, I will surprise you
with a peach hanging from
a low branch in that other mansión

you will never be hungry again
endless milk from my breasts and
a peach to lull you in that eternal sleep

Mansión: heaven

By: Vibiana Aparicio-Chamberlin

"Mother and Child From Gaza." Haiku, poetsonsite https://www.coloradoboulevard.net/ 2025.

"Mother and Child From Gaza." The Southern California Haiku Study Group Anthology, 2025.

return home: human serotiny

piles of rubble give way
to blast riddled homes

operating rooms covered in shrapnel & hate

people (with families alive & dead)
blistered hands thick with dust

bend down to pick up the pieces

burnt photos
a child's toy

ash covered
fire touched

people (with homes standing & fallen)
blistered hands thick with ash

bend down to pick up the pieces

no tears of loss or longing
no time to mourn what was

yesterday's fire released
today's seeds

By: Cherice Cameron

Raza 4 Gaza

The atrocities in Gaza
grow in my hair
to remind all my raza
We are interconnected
in todo lo que pasa–

everything that happens–
shakes through the walls
of your casa.
Our house.
Our Kali.
We need to weave
our familial mat to welcome
Home refugees and work
with the limited abundance
of our daring dreams.

Anarchy has left the shores of impossibility
and demands we see
It's growing out of cracked
Motherlands like weeds
I trust in flow, as it leads
I trust our soul as it bleeds.

and its love is bursting every seam
of this keffiyeh soaked in
an enemy's misdeeds.

There is an unyielding scream
Like a child freshly born-
or a mother on her knees
to prove that life; unlike these bombs
Can never be ceased

By: Josue Emmanuel Muñoz

Protests in Italy: CONTRO IL GENOCIDIO!
ie:Father's Argue With Brave Daughters Because of…

fear
boils continental

daughters protest. fight exhaustion.
fuel for another night of tear gas

hold vigil down Italian roadways
hold signs angry. tired arms do not drop.

daughters walk fearless
fathers weep. come home to safety.

daughters walk fearless
arms of dead flowers & milk

poured in eyes to stop burning buildings
in Palestine

knowing mothers walk alone
in Gaza streets. ghost eyes lolling in empty faces.

knees bloodied. fingertips bloodied.
brothers try to hold back

mother wail
& their own tears

as sisters writhe against hands
unable to comfort another loss

By: Cherice Cameron

Will the Real Wetback, Please Stand Up

There are no beautiful homes set ablaze
No sightings of emergency planes hovering over dry hills of overgrown grass and shrubs
There are no earthquakes
no rubble or crooked rebars erupting from concrete
there are no groups of young men breaking and entering
Or looting department stores
There are no mudslides that are destroying beautiful mansions in the hills

but in the middle of urban cities
among zooming cars and busy streets
adjacent to food trucks
and popular corners

Young men in uniforms
ski masks
handcuffs or zip ties and guns
roaming neighborhoods
and cruising the parking lots
are the new threat
terrorizing innocent men and women

so, let's high five the ICE officers
and give them praise and a raise
for making the streets safe
for pummeling a man
          his face on the hot asphalt
zip-tying his hands behind his back
for tackling a pregnant woman to the ground
for terrifying a young girl on her way to school
who was thinking of the blue skies and mathematics
when they snatched her mother from the sidewalk

They are rounding up Mexicans
like herding cattle and sheep
hauling em away in unmarked vehicles with dark, tinted windows
stuffing them in overcrowded cages

because who needs a delicious meal
or their car washed
or their homes remodeled or repaired
or their yards tended and cared for
or their schools and libraries cleaned
or their children baby sat

who needs strawberries or oranges

And who craves a glass of Chardonnay or Pinot Grigio
because who really likes grapes anyways
or Sunday brunch and all you can drink mimosas

But do not ask me to stand for the Pledge of Allegiance
or to sing the Star-Spangled Banner
or celebrate with fireworks on fourth of July
because there are conditions on my independence
and citizenship don't mean shit

And let me remind you . . .

no one is illegal on stolen land
there is no terrain that cannot be trekked
the sea cannot be held back
there is no fence that cannot be climbed
there is no river that cannot be swam

there is no border on indigenous land
no pencil lines on maps can define territory
this land belongs to the people of the earth
the people of the sun

my brothers and sisters detained by ICE
have been here for thousands of years

you sailed across the Atlantic Ocean only recently -
so, who is the real wetback?

So will the real wetback, please stand up?

By: Donato Martinez

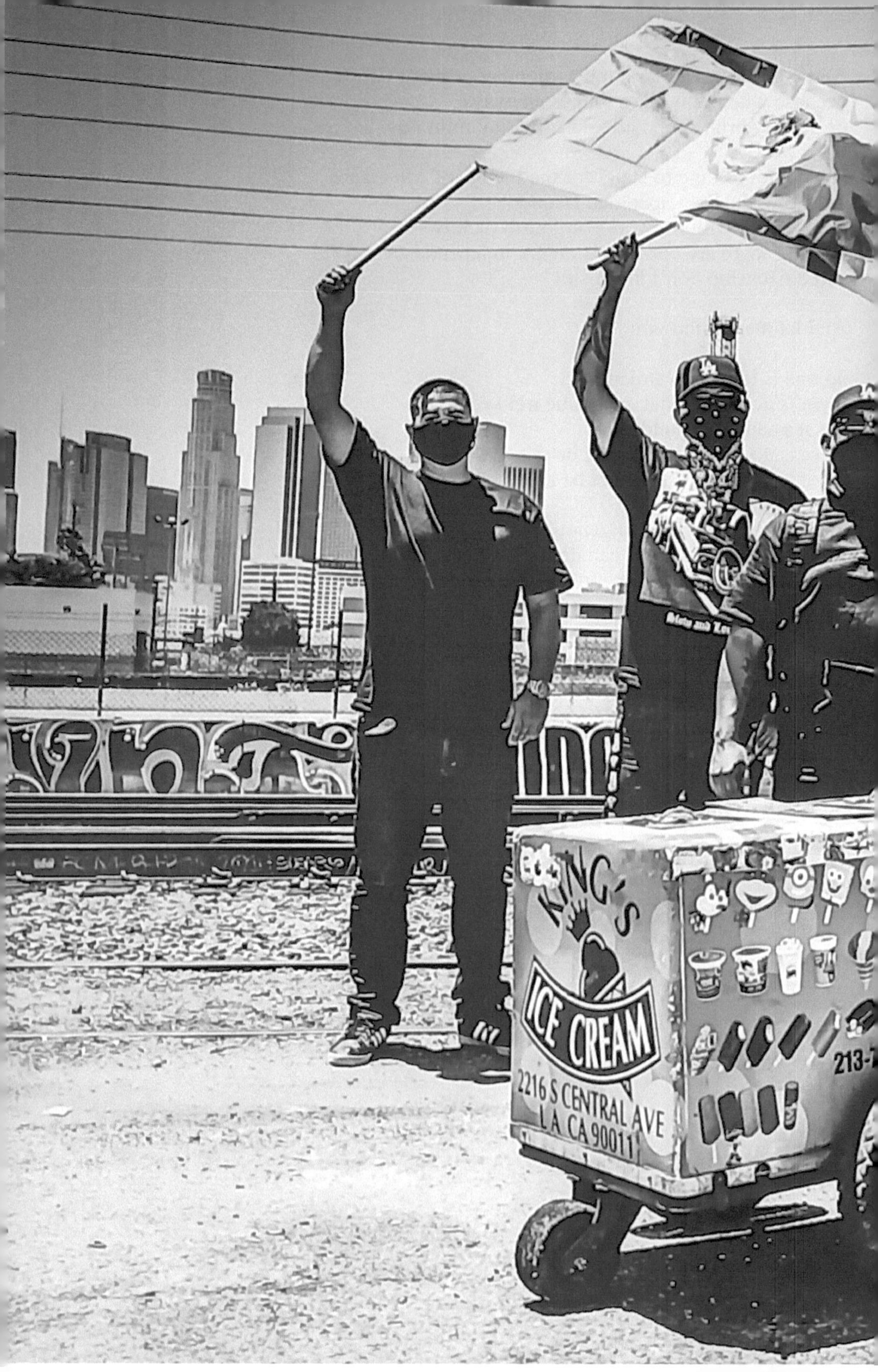
KING'S
ICE CREAM
2216 S CENTRAL AVE
LA CA 90011

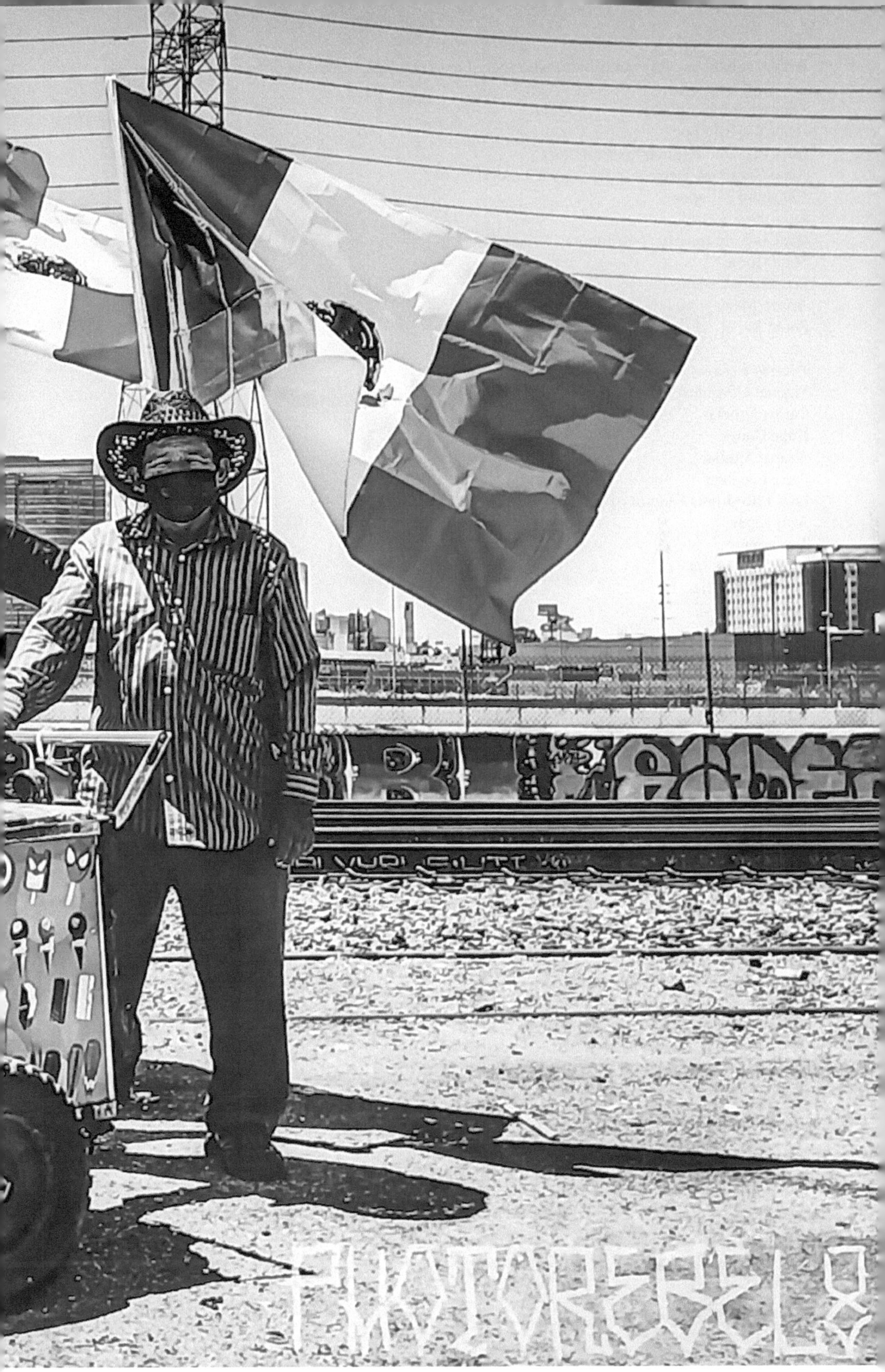

With gratitude to every contributor who shared their courage. Names in order of appearance

Photography and Art
Dante Castro Lopez
Gina Rae Duran (poetry contributor)
Anna Goodman Herrick (poetry contributor)
Alejandra J. Lopez
Joe Crowley
Gia Civerolo (poetry contributor)
Sofia Gomez
Leonard J. Carrillo
Arturo Meza
Photo Rebel

Poetry/ Essays
Manuel Gonzalez New Mexico's Poet Laureate
Carlos Ornelas
Hope Cerna
Azalea Aguilar
Peter Lechuga
Luis J. Rodriguez author of *Always Running*
Aruj Khan
Tezozomoc
Milo Santamaria
Metzli Vik Villa
Anonymous1
Conor Keating
Diosa X
Joe Z
Alex Lorenzen
Vibiana Aparicio-Chamberlin
Claudia Ramirez Flores
VOTH
Donato Martinez
Gina La Valiente
Joe Z
Jake Teran
Katherine Preza Lenore
Ely Lupe
Miguel Lopez President of Chicano Moratorium
Samantha "Sammy" Herrera
Andres RHIPS Rivera
Clara Ximena Roque-Wagner
Oscar Sandoval
Margaret Elysia Garcia
Chrstianne Williams-Vigil
Maestro DeSean
Meliza Bañales
Maria Duarte
Erica Castro
Jamie Maxwell
Jesse Tovar
David Romero
Sandy Shakes
Victor Payan
Jose Emmanuel Muñoz
Cherice Cameron

www.ingramcontent.com/pod-product-compliance
Ingram Content Group UK Ltd.
Pitfield, Milton Keynes, MK11 3LW, UK
UKHW041638190726
13854UKWH00006B/2577

9 781966 337331